Dear Reader:

Charles E. Spicer, Jr.
Executive Editor, St. Martin's True Crime Library

HOUSE OF EVIL
THE INDIANA TORTURE SLAYING

John Dean

St. Martin's Paperbacks

HOUSE OF EVIL

Copyright © 2008 John Dean.

Cover photo of house © *The Indianapolis Star.* Cover photo of Sylvia Likens © Bettmann / Corbis.

All rights reserved.

For information address St. Martin's Press, 175 Fifth Avenue, New York, NY 10010.

ISBN: 0-312-94699-6
EAN: 978-0-312-94699-9

Printed in the United States of America

St. Martin's Paperbacks edition / August 2008

St. Martin's Paperbacks are published by St. Martin's Press, 175 Fifth Avenue, New York, NY 10010.

10 9

Acknowledgments

Bill Brennan, Kimeral Bush, Jill Costill, Tom Fox, Paul A. Kaiser, Dick Roberts, Dan Shreffler, Phil Smith, the Indianapolis Police Department, the Indianapolis and Marion County Public Library, and the Indiana State Library.

Contents

Foreword to the First Edition,
by Leroy K. New, Chief Trial Deputy to Marion
County (Indiana) Prosecutor (1966)

SINCE SELF-PRESERVATION is the most urgent law of nature, it may seem difficult to understand why Sylvia Likens neither sensed nor avoided her impending death. I have no intention of discussing facts or culpability in the matter because the convictions are still on appeal. But I have been repeatedly asked why Sylvia did not just simply run away. I would suggest that by the time Sylvia told her sister she knew she was dying, she had reached profound apathy and had lost all will to resist. She failed to avoid continued abuse because she had no known source of help. Why she did not inform her parents of at least some of her abuse the last time she saw them must remain a silent mystery known only to Sylvia. She may have been painfully disappointed upon learning she could not go with them. Youngsters often sulk and say nothing when disappointed.

But what of Jenny, her sister? In her case, I feel the answer to why she didn't tell someone is quite easy: Fear. She was intensely afraid even to go to her grandmother's home three miles away for fear she'd be thrashed and beaten; and as time passed she assumed a silent, passive attitude, much as prisoners of war who feel it is better to say nothing and know nothing. Neither child could write or otherwise make contact with the parents, for the parents were constantly on the road. A secretly mailed letter was simply out of the question. Then, too, environment and conditions play powerful roles in all human behavior.

If ghetto living produces revolution, it is quite possible that it also produces murder. Legally, such living standards could never justify murder and, indeed, there really is no relation between poverty and bestiality. Poverty itself is not a cause of crime. If it were, we could eliminate crime simply by tearing down tenements and replacing them with elaborate housing projects. The theory does not hold water. We have mounting crime today amid mounting affluence.

But the minds of men do react to agitation and turmoil. The turbulence of pounding pavements and roaring traffic could drive people to unreasonable behavior if they did not try to condition themselves or seek mental tranquility elsewhere. Sylvia accepted Christ. She reached out for a pillar on which to lean. Jenny did the same. They often went forward to the altar together. But at times, it seemed, the entire neighborhood turned on Sylvia. Why? She was gentle by nature and kind to them. Could it be that a national attitude or psychology of the times has eroded and distorted human values to the terrible extent that this generation rewards indolence, exalts muggers, tolerates murder and encourages people to believe they have some proprietary right to other people's properties and, indeed, even their very lives? If so, we are engulfed in a massive moral breakdown that generates civil disobedience and promotes elastic tolerance of wrongdoers.

Thus, to those removed from Sylvia's environment, what happened is shocking and senseless. To those caught up in it, it simply may be a way of life. That way of life may now be on trial also. And if the Sylvia Likens story reflects the moral course America now follows, I say calmly and deliberately that we are on the road to oblivion as a nation. We are free, as citizens, only because every other citizen is restrained from the invasion of the rights of others. Unless we tighten up fast on the reins of law enforcement and restore respect for its purpose in a free society, we will surely experience not liberty, but license as it exists in the jungle, and with the anarchist and the assassin.

In twenty years of the practice of law, in serving three prosecutors and handling homicides totaling well over a hundred, I feel that the Likens story has the most ominous moral implications of any in which I have ever been involved or even heard of. I trust it will serve as a beacon to Americans and even to the world. Ignore it and we are all doomed. Sylvia Likens may speak far louder in death than she ever did while she lived.

Leroy K. New
1966

Editor's note (1966): Leroy K. New holds a law degree from the Indiana University Law School and was admitted to practice in Indiana in 1946 and in

Florida in 1947. He is a member of the Indianapolis Bar Association, the Florida State Bar Association, and the Indiana Prosecutors Association. He is a frequent lecturer at the Indiana University Law School and is widely experienced in criminal law. He has assisted grand juries in investigations of the Indianapolis Coliseum explosion, a gambling scandal involving Indianapolis police officers, vice in Indianapolis, and control of obscene publications. He is married and the father of two daughters, 12 and 15 years of age.

Author's Preface to the New Edition

THE ORIGINAL edition of this book sold more than 55,000 copies in 1966 and 1967, and I was surprised. I was a newspaper reporter, and I knew that I was reporting a big story that had been broadcast around the world; but I had this lingering wonderment at who would want to read so much about it.

While I was reporting on the Sylvia Likens murder case for the *Indianapolis Star*, I fantasized about writing a book on it. I shared my dream with a writer for *Time* magazine who was covering the case, and he agreed that it would be a good idea. But I did not send out a book proposal to agents or publishers. I was *commissioned* to write the book—by David Zentner, the publisher of Bee-Line Books Inc., then of Cleveland, Ohio (later of New York).

Only after the book was published did I realize that Bee-Line's main line had been pornography. My book and another published the same year—*Viet Nam Mission to Hell!*, by Val Seran—were Bee-Line's entrées into the publishing mainstream. Previous titles in the company's catalog included such titles as *Peekin' Place*, *Some Came Sinning* and *In Hot Blood*.

What really surprised me, though—much more than the initial sales—was that the book became a "cult classic." Long after it went out of print (the first printing was 75,000 copies, and they did not sell out), I kept getting queries from people from all over the country and a few from overseas—by mail and by telephone—asking where they could get a copy (this began long before eBay and AbeBooks.com came around).

A few of the queries came from playwrights, filmmakers and television writers (two women in New York said they had connections with Bill Moyers and wanted to produce a documentary). Sadly, I told them all, the book was out of print (I made photocopies of my last, dog-eared copy of the book for some of the writers).

A student at Indiana State University—who was not from Indiana, but from the Southwest—visited me to examine my archives in order to write a term paper about the case.

The oddball movie director John Waters published an essay in which he fantasized about getting a copy of *The Indiana Torture Slaying* in his Christmas stocking.

What *is* it about this case? I wondered.

And to one of my many correspondents I mused, "I wish I knew who owned the copyright on that book."

"Who does own the copyright?" he asked.

Light bulb! I didn't know. But I knew enough copyright law to realize that the original copyright had expired; and I hired a copyright lawyer in Washington, D.C., to find out who owned the renewal rights.

"You do!" he wrote back, in so many words, after a little research. So I republished the book myself, in 1999, and printed it myself, under the imprint of a small press I had founded in 1980, and it has sold steadily ever since. I made more money on the first hundred copies I published myself than I did as the author on the 55,000 copies that had been sold more than thirty years before.

And now, finally, a Hollywood movie has been made about the case—*An American Crime*, which debuted at the 2007 Sundance Film Festival.

But all this merely *demonstrates* the continuing fascination with the murder of Sylvia Likens by Gertrude Baniszewski and a gang of children. It doesn't *explain* the fascination. And I remain at a loss to explain it.

Many writers, including the writer and director of *An American Crime*, have compared the Likens case to William Golding's 1954 novel *Lord of the Flies*, in which a community of unsupervised children commit unspeakable atrocities on their fellows.

But that comparison has never convinced me. The children in *Lord of the Flies* had no adult supervision. The children who participated in the murder of Sylvia Likens were not merely sanctioned, but were even directed, by an adult—the divorcee Gertrude Baniszewski. I find the Sylvia Likens murder more comparable to the murders committed by the minions of Charles Manson than to the murders in *Lord of the Flies*.

I have received compliments over the years for

the straightforward narrative of *The Indiana Torture Slaying*, but I have taken some criticism for not explaining why that divorcee and those children would commit such a crime, and why the Likens girls did not flee. I have three things to say about that.

First, I'm not a psychologist, and I was not asked by my publisher to pretend to be one. In fact, it was not really clear to me what the publisher wanted when he commissioned me to write the book. I sent him a manuscript within a month of the verdict, based principally on the trial, and he sent it right back. "No, no," he said. "Have you read *In Cold Blood*?" (Truman Capote's seminal "true crime" novel, published the year before.)

"No," I confessed.

"Read it," he said. "And then send me another manuscript. That's what I want."

I did, and I did; and now you have it.

So, that's the first thing I have to say: Just the facts, ma'am.

Second: There's a book on the Internet about the case, at crimelibrary.com, by Denise Noe, a writer in Atlanta. The title of one of the chapters of her e-book is "The Sexless Sex Crime." Her point was that, although Sylvia's tormentors accused her of sexual misconduct and forced her to masturbate with a Pepsi-Cola bottle, there was no evidence that any of them had personally sexually assaulted or molested her.

But I disagreed that the Sylvia Likens crime was "sexless," and I e-mailed Ms. Noe and argued with her about that title (we have since become friends). I pointed out that Ricky Hobbs, age 14 at the time of the murder, was not a friend of the Baniszewski children. He was a friend of Gertrude Baniszewski. He even said so, to both the police and the coroner's investigator. That and other sexual innuendos, including defense attorneys' portrayal of Gertrude Baniszewski as a siren, were reported in the articles I wrote for the *Indianapolis Star* at the time as well as in my book.

There's a photograph of Gertrude Baniszewski and Ricky Hobbs in court together that is worth a thousand words. It shows Baniszewski and Hobbs *as a couple*. It's one of the most remarkable journalistic photos you will ever see. In my mind it ranks with the 1930s photos of the Okies, with the 1945 Iwo Jima photo, and with the photo of the young girl running toward the camera, and away from the napalm, in Viet Nam. I don't know who took the courtroom photo of Gertrude and Ricky. I saw it in a detective magazine, uncredited and uncopyrighted.

There was a sexual relationship between Ricky Hobbs and Gertrude Baniszewski. I am not saying that they had sexual relations. Only they would know that, and both are deceased. Hobbs denied it vehemently on the witness stand (Gertrude Baniszewski was not asked). But denial is fiercest in the face of circumstantial evidence impossible to rebut. I have reservations about the credibility of Hobbs' denial. What else besides sex would motivate an otherwise decent young man to carve words upon a girl's belly with a burning wand? Everything fits—including Hobbs' death at 21 years of age from cancer. He was a tormented young man.

So, there's a little psychology for you. All I am saying is that sex is a powerful enough motivation for murder. We know that from history. Sex was Charles Manson's most powerful persuasion of the young women who killed for him (and of the men who killed for him, too, rewarded by sexual favors from his women).

But while we can speculate forever on Ricky Hobbs' motivation in the murder of Sylvia Likens, and on the others', we'll never know.

Third: The prosecutor, Leroy New, presented the best psychological analysis of the crime I have ever seen, in his introduction to the first edition of this book, reprinted in this edition. He dealt harshly with the defense's excuse of poverty, and intensively with Sylvia Likens' failure to avoid or escape her fate. He makes as good a case with that as he made in court.

This book presents the facts of the case. You figure it out.

John Dean
2008

Revised Author's Preface
to the First Edition

IN ALMOST every trial, the 12 members of the jury are faced with the task of sifting the truth out of hours of conflicting testimony. They must decide what is right, what is wrong; what is significant, what is trivial; who is truthful, who is lying; who remembers correctly, who has forgotten. Even the honest witness unconsciously distorts facts in the retelling. To reconstruct what actually did happen in each detail, from the testimony, is impossible. The juror can only come to a reasonable conclusion as to what happened.

This book is an attempt to come to a reasonable conclusion as to what actually happened to Sylvia Likens. The reader is spared the task of sifting through reams of conflicting testimony, much of it purposely distorted. The conclusions of this book, which is in narrative form, are based on a selection of the most credible testimony in a five-week trial, on statements that eyewitnesses gave to police and to writers outside the trial, on the opinions of lawyers, on the interpretations of psychiatrists, and on the confirmation of a jury's verdict.

Some incidents related in this book may not have occurred exactly as they are told. That a perfect reconstruction of the brutal crime would be achieved was neither expected nor intended, for it would have been impossible. The book represents an honest attempt to present a reasonable reconstruction of the crime in a readable form.

John Dean
1966

Principal Characters

Gertrude Baniszewski, alias Gertrude Wright, 37 years old, charged with murder

Her children, Paula Baniszewski, 17; Stephanie Baniszewski, 15; and Johnny Baniszewski, 12, all charged with murder; and Marie Baniszewski, 11; Shirley Baniszewski, 10; Jimmy Baniszewski, 8, and Dennis Lee Wright Jr., 1

Richard (Ricky) Hobbs, 14, a neighbor, charged with murder

Coy Hubbard, 15, a neighbor and Stephanie's boyfriend, charged with murder

Sylvia Likens, 16 years old, the victim, daughter of carnival workers and a boarder in Mrs. Baniszewski's house

Jenny Likens, 15, Sylvia's sister, also a boarder with Mrs. Baniszewski

Lester Likens, 39, and Betty Likens, 37, Sylvia and Jenny's parents

Sgt. William E. Kaiser, Indianapolis Police homicide detective

Leroy K. New and Marjorie Wessner, Marion County (Indiana) deputy prosecutors

William C. Erbecker, attorney for Mrs. Baniszewski; George P. Rice Jr., attorney for Paula; John R. Hammond, attorney for Stephanie; Forrest B. Bowman Jr., attorney for Johnny and for Coy Hubbard; James G. Nedeff, attorney for Richard Hobbs

Saul I. Rabb, trial judge

1

"THE MOST TERRIBLE CRIME"

TWO CHILDREN—A boy and a girl in their early teens—knelt over the motionless body of another teenage girl, trying to breathe life back into her mangled, emaciated form. They were trying to deny what was already, but for a few last, labored breaths, a fact. A deputy prosecutor was later to call this death "the most terrible crime ever committed in the state of Indiana."

"She's faking! She's all right!" screeched the haggard, panic-stricken woman standing in the doorway.

The boy, a gangly 14-year-old whose straight blond hair tended to slide over his black horn-rimmed glasses, rushed the woman back downstairs.

"Someone better call a doctor or somebody," his companion told him when he regained the top of the stairs. Stephanie Baniszewski, 15 years old, had never looked more serious. A glint of reproach in her eyes told Richard Hobbs that she meant it.

He started back down, taking the last three steps in one jump. Stephanie heard her mother, the woman who had been forced downstairs, tell Richard that the police were the ones to call. The Hobbs boy, joined by the woman's husky 12-year-old son Johnny, headed for the nearest telephone—a pay phone at the Shell station across the corner. It was at twilight of what had been a brisk October day, but the boys knew they had no time to put on wraps before darting across the busy one-way street.

Patrolman Melvin D. Dixon had been cruising the neighborhood about two hours when the radio crackled with his signal. He saw no reason to expect any particular trouble on this night. It was a Tuesday, and it was chilly. It had been quiet so far, except for the usual rush-hour headaches. The traffic had slacked off now, and since it was not quite dark yet, Dixon thought he would have things easy for a while. Lean, dark, and roughly handsome in his dark blue uniform, Dixon, 45 years old, had been on the force long enough to know you sometimes get trouble when you least expect it, however.

It was 6:27 p.m., October 26, 1965, when the dispatcher called Dixon's signal. "Go—to—3850 East New York," the dispatcher spaced out the words in his usual casual manner. "Investigate possible dead girl."

You don't get one like that every day. But then, more often than not, it turns out to be a fainting spell; occasionally a child might bleed to death from a household cut.

But Dixon had heard the homicide car being radioed to the scene too, along with other patrol cars;

and any "possible dead" calls rated prompt attention, he knew, for the simple fact it might not be too late for resuscitation. He was there in minutes.

The door was open; he walked in. The haggard woman, wan and drawn for her 37 years, met him. He talked to her long enough to take down her name—"Gertrude Wright, white, female, 37"—and the name of the girl—"Sylvia Likens, white, female, 16." Mrs. Wright handed him a note and showed him upstairs, telling him the girl had wandered into her backyard bare-breasted an hour before, clutching the note. The girl had been a boarder at her home, Mrs. Wright said, but had run off with a gang of boys several days before.

The note, on a sheet of lined notebook paper in a childish scrawl, said:

To Mr. and Mrs. Likens:

I went with a gang of boys in the middle of the night. And they said that they would pay me if I would give them something so I got in the car and they all got what they wanted and they did and did and when they got finished they beat me up and left sores on my face and all over my body.

And they also put on my stomach, I am a prostitute and proud of it.

I have done just about everything that I could do just to make Gertie mad and ~~cause~~ cost Gertie more money than she's got. I've

*tore up a new mattress and peaed on it. I have
also cost Gertie doctor bills that she really
can't pay and made Gertie a nervous wreck
and all her kids. I cost her $35.00 for a hospi-
tal in one day and I wouldn't do nothing around
the house. I have done anything to do things to
make things out of the way to make things
worse for them.*

This pitiful note was not signed. Had Dixon
taken the time to read it then, he would have suspected it was phony, merely from the formal form
of address from a girl to her parents. He would
have seen that the note no doubt was dictated by
someone else, from the writer's mistaking the
sound of "cost" in the third paragraph for "cause,"
as is apparent in the correction made. But Dixon,
who later handed the note to a detective, was more
intent on seeing the body.

What he saw was the long, thin body of a teenage
girl stretched out on her back on a mattress on the
floor of the bedroom. Although she wore sweater
and slacks, her midriff was exposed, and Dixon
could plainly see the words "I'M A PROSTITUTE AND
PROUD OF IT!" freshly carved on her belly. Above
that inscription, deeply branded into her chest, was a
large, curious "3." Her light brown hair was shaggy,
disheveled and cut short. Her face was covered with
sores, and the entire left side of her face was discolored where the skin had eroded. There were open

sores also around the markings on her abdomen, and bruises. Dixon knew that she was dead.

The deputy coroner, Dr. Arthur Paul Kebel, arrived about an hour later. He found the body in complete rigor and at room temperature, indicating she may have been dead eight hours. But he also noted that she had been bathed recently, perhaps after death, and that the water could have lowered the body temperature quicker; he knew also that prolonged shock before death can quicken rigor mortis and loss of heat.

The 47-year-old physician examined the body thoroughly, observing a few things the policeman had missed. There was a large bruise on the left side of the head, about the temple. A tooth was missing. Cuts, burns and scald marks covered the body; the numerous patches where skin had eroded seemed to have been caused by scalding water or acid. The body was covered also with more than 100 small, round sores—"punctate wounds," the doctor called them. One was a hole almost to the bone, on her right wrist. Each "punctate wound" was about the size and shape of the end of a cigarette.

The vagina was swollen and puffy. On the girl's back was a discolored, bruised area about the size of a hand. The sores were in various stages of healing.

The skinny, distraught matron of the house hovered about Dr. Kebel as he examined the girl's body, explaining that she had applied rubbing alcohol as first aid.

Kebel was surprised to find no evidence of sexual molestation other than the swollen pubic region.

Also hovering about the doctor, jabbering away, was the Hobbs boy. "What are you doing here?" the doctor demanded.

"I'm a neighbor and a friend of Gertie's," he said.

Kebel was shocked and confused. He suspected no one around him. He assumed the murder to be the work of some anonymous madman.

Dr. Charles R. Ellis, the young resident pathologist who performed the autopsy on the girl's body a few hours later, noticed a few more things. Her lips were in shreds; her fingernails were broken backward, all of them. Though not yet 30, Ellis was a veteran of more than 250 criminal autopsies; but he cringed as he thought of the pain Sylvia had endured.

Ellis noted that the patchy skin-loss areas were mainly about the face, neck and breasts; the right knee also was bare of skin.

Examination of the internal organs revealed more. The liver was fatty and yellow, indicating malnutrition (the pelvic bones' prominence also indicated loss of weight). An alteration in the kidneys indicated the victim had been in shock for some time prior to her death, perhaps as much as two or three days. Examination of the brain showed the effect of the large external bruise about the temple. The doctor drained off two tablespoons of free-flowing, unclotted blood. Unstopped bleeding in such an area causes loss of consciousness and eventually death as pressure on the brain builds up. The doctor concluded that Sylvia died of a "subdural hematoma" caused by the blow to the head, with shock, malnutrition and the excessive injuries as underlying factors.

DETECTIVE SGT. William E. Kaiser had arrived at the Wright home within 10 minutes of Patrolman Dixon. Other policemen already were swarming through the house, taking photographs, making notes and controlling traffic.

Shortly after Kaiser's arrival, a tiny teenage girl limped toward the house from across New York Street. A rake in her hand, her dingy blond hair stringing from her shoulders, the crippled girl quickened her pace as she saw the patrol cars parked outside the house. A wave of anxiety swept across her face. Her shriveled left leg was encased in a steel brace, but she broke into a near trot as she neared the home.

Police reports listed her later as Jenny Fay Likens, white, female, 15. Sylvia was her sister.

Jenny burst into the front room. Someone said Sylvia was dead. Tears streamed down the polio victim's face.

Arriving about the same time, home from her job at a neighborhood cafeteria, was a large, brown-haired, slovenly, bottle-bottomed girl named Paula. She was 17, Mrs. Wright's eldest daughter. She, too, heard the news that Sylvia had died. "You're kidding!" she exclaimed.

They were not kidding. Paula reached for her Bible. She began reading to Jenny. "This was meant to happen," she intoned then, softly. "If you want to live with us, Jenny, we'll treat you like our own sister."

Mrs. Wright came into the room, bustling about like a busy stage director. "Did you tell them I'd been doctoring Sylvia?" she reminded.

Jenny remembered her lines: No one had seen Sylvia for several days; she had run off with a gang of boys; she staggered into the backyard at 5:30 p.m., bare-breasted, clutching a note. But Jenny ad-libbed, also. "You get me out of here," she whispered to a policeman, "and I'll tell you everything."

By 9 p.m., several members of the household were on their way downtown. Richard Hobbs, who had been allowed to go home, was rousted out of bed and hustled into a paddy wagon. The wagon was halfway to police headquarters in the 26-story City-County Building, but it backtracked for one more passenger—12-year-old Johnny Baniszewski.

Grim detectives unlocked the doors in the homicide office and went to work. Kaiser, a large, middle-aged, red-faced man, his speech slow and measured, had the appearance of a rube. But he had been a policeman and a homicide detective a long time. He sensed what was up.

He spoke first with Jenny Likens. Next he talked with Richard Hobbs.

"You are in serious trouble," he told the boy. "I

know that girl didn't die at the hands of five boys. Do you want to call your dad before you talk to me?"

Ricky knew his father was worried enough about his wife, Ricky's mother, who was dying of cancer in Community Hospital. He decided to face the veteran detective alone.

Next Detective Kaiser talked to Mrs. Wright. He learned that her true name was Baniszewski, the same as that of six of her seven children; that her brief cohabitation with 20-year-old Dennis Lee Wright, father of her youngest child, had not been sanctioned by law.

Mrs. Baniszewski handed Kaiser, from her purse, another letter from Sylvia to her parents, on school tablet paper and longer than the note Sylvia supposedly clutched as she staggered into the backyard. It began, "Mom and Dad," and it was signed, "Sylvia Likens."

It listed 15 confessions of theft, sexual adventure and other misbehavior: "I am writing to tell you what I have done for the last two weeks. . . . I done things that could cause a lot of trouble. . . . I took $10 from Gertie Wright. . . ."

The handwriting may have been authentic, but Kaiser knew the motivation was not. By this time he was irritated. He brusquely informed Mrs. Baniszewski that she was under arrest on a preliminary charge of murder and that she might contact an attorney if she chose.

By midnight, Mrs. Baniszewski and Richard Dean Hobbs were in custody on murder charges.

Three of Mrs. Baniszewski's children and five neighbor children were taken into custody within the next few days on juvenile delinquency charges. They were Paula Marie Baniszewski, 17; Stephanie Kay Baniszewski, 15; John Stephan Baniszewski Jr., 12; Stephanie's boyfriend, Coy Randolph Hubbard, 15; Randy Gordon Lepper, 12; Judy Darlene Duke, 12; Anna Ruth Siscoe, 13, and Michael John Monroe, 11.

By the end of the year, after a grand jury investigation, Mrs. Baniszewski, Paula, Stephanie, Johnny, Hobbs and Hubbard were being held in jail without bond on charges of first-degree murder. The other four children had been released to their parents, under subpoena as state's witnesses. The stage was set for the most searing courtroom drama in Indiana history.

2

THEY DIDN'T PRY

IT WAS a hot July day in Indianapolis. The early afternoon sun beat down heavily on New York Street, a busy one-way thoroughfare bearing impatient traffic from the frustrating vehicle snarls downtown.

Many of the motorists, who traveled the route every day on their way home from work to fashionable East Side homes, harbored a mild curiosity about life on East New York Street. Teenage children wearing frayed tennis shoes and small fry in their underwear frolicked on the sidewalks, darting in and out of the small business establishments that dotted the neighborhood.

Weary, sweating adults sometimes leaned out the windows of their homes that were jammed tightly against the sidewalks, gazing at the children or the noisy tide of traffic.

An exciting life it must be, the motorists thought, retaining their preference for the gentler life.

Had they stopped to investigate, they would have

found a somewhat gentler life in that very neighborhood. Though New York Street itself was lined with rotting rental houses divided into apartments, side streets boasted modest, clean, well-kept homes of a generally blue-collar population—carpenters, laborers, policemen, a few teachers, an occasional lawyer or chiropractor. Most owned their own homes. The finger streets supported a stable neighborhood.

This particular day, the motorists might have seen three young girls, about high school age, strolling the sidewalk of New York Street. They would not have known the girls; this was a city of half a million. Unlike the people of most Hoosier communities, the residents of the Hoosier capital are city minded; they know few of their neighbors and still fewer outside their own neighborhoods.

These three girls happened to be two sisters and their best friend in the neighborhood; their names were Sylvia Likens, Jenny Likens and Darlene McGuire; their ages 16, 15, and 14 years, respectively.

They were happy. They kept up with the popular tunes; they talked about boys; they liked to skate and dance—that is, except for Jenny. Her skating and dancing were limited by a shriveled left leg in a steel brace, but she had learned to live with this from the age of four months, and she could keep up with her companions. And despite her deformity, she was not unattractive, so she could talk about boys, too.

The Likens girls had no particular reason to be happy, except that they were children and were with a friend. Their mother had been arrested for shoplifting. That had never happened before. Their mother and father were separated. That had happened before. Since they were in the custody of their mother—their father residing in his hometown, the small city of Lebanon, 30 miles to the northwest— they were alone. That had happened before, too, and there was a certain amount of adventure and excitement in being unsupervised.

The Likens girls had just moved into the neighborhood a couple of weeks before, when their mother rented an apartment at 109 North Euclid Avenue, two blocks off New York Street. Before the parents' separation, the family had just returned from three months in Long Beach, Calif., where Lester Likens had worked for Douglas Aircraft. The girls and their two brothers had liked the West Coast, but their parents were homesick, so they had returned to Lebanon, where Sylvia was born.

The neighborhood was not unfamiliar. The house at 3838 East New York Street—now the home of the Monroe family—was one of the fourteen homes in and around Indianapolis in which the Likens family had resided since the 1944 teenage marriage of Lester and his Indianapolis sweetheart, who herself had grown up on the East Side. Likens had never done particularly well, drifting from job to job, but he had always managed to eke out a living, sometimes with welfare help from the township trustee.

Darlene knew a family in this same block of New York Street with seven children. Gertrude Wright and her brood lived here, at 3850 East New York Street. The girls stopped in. Sylvia had no idea then that she would never get out.

She and Jenny made friends quickly with Mrs. Wright's daughters, the Baniszewski girls. They asked Sylvia and Jenny to stay for supper. That is, Mrs. Wright asked Jenny. Jenny said yes, but not unless Sylvia could stay, too. She was puzzled that the woman's invitation had not included Sylvia.

They returned to their mother's apartment after they had eaten. Jenny reminisced on the events of the day. She and Sylvia and their mother had been on their way to Rollerland, about 10:30 that morning. Mommy said she was too warm in her black slacks. It was a hot day—Saturday, July 3, 1965. Children already were popping firecrackers as Jenny and Sylvia sat alone in the second-floor apartment.

The girls and their mother stopped into a discount house on East 10th Street, Jenny remembered. Mommy had tried on a pair of shorts or pedal-pushers—Jenny could not remember which now, even though she and Sylvia had been in the dressing room with their mother. They thought she was going to buy them, but Betty Likens just stuffed the shorts or pedal-pushers into her purse and strolled toward the door.

"Come on, Sylvia," Jenny said. "Let's get to the other side of the store. I don't want to be with her when she does anything like that." They left the store through another doorway and waited for their mother on a bench outside. Mrs. Likens had barely exited when her arm was grabbed by a woman floor-walker.

Mommy was hustled back inside and forced to empty the contents of her purse. Out fell the stolen merchandise. Before being driven away in the paddy wagon, Mrs. Likens gave her daughters $2 from her billfold, saying, "Get something to eat."

We were foolish to spend 70 cents of it on ice cream sodas, Jenny thought. It was lucky Mrs. Wright asked us to stay for supper.

Before the girls went for a walk with Darlene, they went to a pay phone to call the Women's Prison and ask for Betty Likens. Their mother was not there, of course.

Now, as the firecrackers popped and darkness descended, Sylvia and Jenny began to feel lonely. They hoped Mommy would be back tomorrow.

The next day, tired of sitting around alone waiting for their mother, the girls went again to Darlene's house. Sylvia and Darlene got into a convertible with another girl, but Jenny chose to stay behind. She went back to her mother's apartment and accepted the landlady's invitation to watch television down-stairs. She was still lonely and was greatly relieved to hear Sylvia's and Darlene's voices outside.

Paula Baniszewski was with them. They set out for her house.

Paula was laughing. "I'm two months pregnant," she said.

"Aw, you're kidding," Jenny said. She did not know Paula.

Darlene asked Sylvia and Jenny if they would like to help her clean house that summer. She said her parents were going to give her $5 a week for it.

Soon the girls arrived at Paula's house. They had Cokes and talked. Two of the Baniszewski children, 12-year-old Johnny and 15-year-old Stephanie, were away on a vacation trip with their divorced and re-married father, John S. Baniszewski Sr., a police-man in the South Side suburb of Beech Grove. But there was no more room in the house than usual. Mrs. Wright's sister-in-law and her two children were staying there then. Though it got noisy at times, their six-room share of the two-story, dingy, gray frame double on the corner was big enough to hold them all.

Sylvia and Jenny were invited to spend the night, and the children stayed up to celebrate Shirley Baniszewski's 10th birthday at midnight.

If Gertrude Wright looked drawn and exhausted, there were reasons, not the least of which were the thirteen pregnancies—and six miscarriages—she had endured. The latest miscarriage had been in the preceding April, and it was complicated by the disappearance soon after of her eldest daughter, Paula, 17, who ran away with a married man to Hazard, Kentucky.

Gertrude had counted on Paula to help her run the house. She was forced to resume taking in iron-ing a few days after her miscarriage in order to keep the family going. By May, she was working as much as sixteen hours a day, ironing, baby-sitting, and vending at the Indianapolis Motor Speedway during the month of the 500 Mile Race.

Gertrude had never had it easy. Her father, whom she adored, died of a heart attack before her very eyes when she was 11 years old. The third of six children and not overly fond of her mother, Gertrude quit school at the age of 16 and soon married John Baniszewski, who was two years older. She clerked in drug stores and dime stores and bore her husband four children.

She divorced him after 10 years, and there followed an unhappy three-month marriage in Kansas to a man named Edward Gutherie, who did not care for the children. Gertrude returned to Indianapolis and lived with her former husband, Baniszewski, for seven more years, bearing him two more children.

She divorced him again in 1963, and began cohabiting with her young lover, Dennis Lee Wright, and bore him a son, Dennis Jr. When he deserted her, she filed paternity suits against him for support of Dennis Jr. and for expenses of the miscarriage. The woman suffered physical abuse at the hands of Wright and perhaps one of her other husbands, and she was a chronic sufferer of asthma and nervous tension. Her chain-smoking complicated her respiratory ailments.

In the summer of 1965, Gertrude—5 feet 6 inches tall but weighing barely 100 pounds—began to feel the pressure she had felt fifteen years before, when she had suffered a nervous breakdown after the birth of Stephanie. She looked at least 10 years older than her 37 years. With her own children, and neighbor children, in and out of the house all day, she had her hands full. But the appearance of the Likens girls, she soon saw, presented an opportunity to supplement her meager income, which at the time consisted of child support payments, payment for ironing, and the few dollars brought in occasionally by Paula, who had returned from her Kentucky spree, disillusioned and only a little wiser.

"How old do you guess my mother is?" asked Paula.

"How old is your oldest daughter?" Jenny asked of Mrs. Wright.

"Paula is 17," she said.

"Then I would say you are 37," Jenny said.

"No," she said, "I'm 31." This "young" woman felt a little tired that night, though, and retired early.

Shortly before midnight, there was a knock at the door. "There are two men out there," said Shirley, peering through the glass in the door.

Jenny took a peek. "It's my daddy and my brother Danny," she exulted.

Lester Likens drew his girls out on the porch before asking, "Where's Mommy?"

"She's in jail," they whispered, not wanting the others to hear.

Likens said he and Danny, 19, had been looking all over for his wife and the girls after finding no one in the Euclid Avenue apartment. Darlene had directed him to the Baniszewski house. Lester said he had plans to go on a tour of Indiana county fairs, to operate a concessions stand with a carnival company, and he wanted "Mommy" to go with him. "You girls get ready," he said. "You're going to Lebanon."

Gertrude was awakened by the sound of male voices. She invited Lester and Danny inside. They left briefly for a quick supper of White Castle hamburgers, which they brought back to the house and shared with Mrs. Wright and her children.

Then Likens and his son continued their search. Jail officials told him his wife had been released. Not finding her at her Euclid Avenue apartment, he returned to Mrs. Wright's, exhausted and somewhat under the influence of liquor. As he sat in the easy chair, he cried, spouting words of love for his wife and his five children. He and Danny accepted Mrs. Wright's offer for them to spend the night in her living room.

Before he fell asleep, Lester talked of his carnival plans. Mrs. Wright saw her opportunity and seized it. She offered to board the girls for $20 a week and treat them like her own. Her own daughters insisted on it, and the Likens girls agreed. Lester gave his tentative approval, pending the approval of his wife.

Jenny and Sylvia that night shared an upstairs bedroom with Marie Baniszewski, 11; Shirley Baniszewski, just turned 10, and Jimmy Baniszewski, 8. The children were to take turns with a bed in the room and a mattress laid out on the floor. That night, Jenny and Sylvia slept on the bed.

Up at daybreak, Lester Likens found his wife at her parents' home at 333 South Temple Avenue, and told her of the carnival plans.

They returned to Mrs. Wright's, and Mrs. Likens agreed to the terms for her daughters. Lester plunked down $20 in advance. Neither he nor his wife so much as inspected the house. Neither had gone beyond the living room; neither knew that there was no stove, but only a hot plate in the kitchen; that there was a shortage of beds upstairs. "I didn't pry," Likens was to testify later. "I was going to let my mother in Lebanon take care of them, but she had her hands full."

"You'll have to take care of these girls with a firm hand," Likens told Mrs. Wright before he left, "because their mother has let them do as they please."

3

THE HONEYMOON ENDS

SYLVIA LIKENS was cute; friends called her Cookie. Her long curly hair hung below her shoulders. She was slender and pretty and in the bloom of life. She had something of a sassy look about her, but that was from keeping her mouth closed, even when she smiled. She was trying to conceal the gap left by a missing front tooth, knocked out in a childhood collision with a brother.

But Sylvia was a generally quiet, unassuming girl, and everyone liked her. She was helpful and gladly pitched in with the housework while the others played that summer at the Baniszewski house, just as she had helped at home, where she also gave her mother part of her earnings from a regular baby-sitting job and from ironing she took in. She was soon to find her housework appreciated about as much as Cinderella's.

Sylvia was no angel, but she was a religious girl. She owned a Bible, and she had been baptized along with her brothers and sisters two years before at the

East 16th Street Christian Church in Indianapolis. Before the summer of 1965 was over, she was to find herself too busy with housework to attend Sunday school.

"Sylvia," a neighbor recounted, "said she felt she was the odd one in the family because she was born between two sets of twins." Danny and Dianna were two years older; Jenny and Benny, a year younger.

Sylvia was neither bright nor stupid. She made average grades in school and passed most of her subjects despite repeated absences. When she turned 16 on January 3, 1965, she quit school as her father, mother, brother and sister had done. But now established at the Baniszewskis', she planned to re-enter Arsenal Technical High School, her mother's alma mater, in September as a freshman.

Sylvia's first week at 3850 East New York Street was pleasant enough. The girls would listen to phonograph records in the house or walk to one of three parks within a three-mile radius. Jenny, steel brace and all, would hobble along with the rest of them.

Mrs. Wright, struggling to pay the $55-a-month rent and keep the family in food, became understandably edgy at times. She would scream at the kids to get out of the house; that's how some of the trips to the park started.

Neighbor children were always around too. Randy Lepper, the mischievous, cherub-faced 12-year-old from across Denny Street (the Baniszewski house was on the corner) dropped in regularly; so did Darlene McGuire. Later, in July, Richard Hobbs, a 14-year-old from two doors north on Denny Street, was introduced to the household. Judy Duke, Anna Siscoe, Mike Monroe and others came over frequently, as the children in the neighborhood got acquainted. The Baniszewskis had occupied the home only several weeks, and already it was becoming a neighborhood center. Jenny's twin brother, Benny, staying with his grandparents, spent two or three nights at the Baniszewski home that summer.

Meals were skimpy, but no one complained. A day's fare might consist of two pieces of toast for breakfast, skipping lunch while at the park all day, and a bowl of soup for supper.

About July 17, Sylvia met the girl who was to become her best friend in the house. Danny was with them too as Mrs. Wright and her children, with Sylvia, took a drive in the children's aunt's car to pick up Stephanie, who was returning to Mrs. Wright. Not until she arose the next morning and saw Sylvia still there, plus Sylvia's sister Jenny, did Stephanie realize there were two additions to the family.

But before Stephanie's arrival, Jenny and Sylvia had gotten a taste of things to come. Mrs. Wright dragged them both upstairs, slapped Jenny, and snarled, "Well, I took care of you two bitches for a week for nothing." The next day a money order from Lester Likens arrived in the mail for his girls' care.

A few days later, Likens and his wife visited their daughters between fairs, and Likens gave Mrs. Wright another $20 in advance. The girls did not complain during their parents' brief visit. Mr. and

Mrs. Likens often stopped by for a half-hour or an hour on weekends if they were home between fairs. When they were in Indianapolis for two weeks at the end of August for the Indiana State Fair, their visits were no more frequent, however.

Sylvia was paddled again the third week in July, when Mrs. Wright became convinced Sylvia was getting the Baniszewski children to loiter about grocery stores, snitching bottles to turn in for deposit return. The Likens girls' father had told them they could pick up a few pennies by finding empty pop bottles to turn in; they spent part of their time in the park looking for bottles.

When Mrs. Wright found out about it from her children, both Jenny and Sylvia "got the board." That means they were whipped with a quarter-inch-thick fraternity-style paddle. If Sylvia was lucky, she got it in the back. Eventually she got it in the back of the head. If Gertrude was feeling weak from her asthma or bronchitis, she would delegate the punishment to Paula, who didn't mind.

It was not to Sylvia's advantage that neighbor children were mobbing the house the fourth week in July, because that irritated Mrs. Wright. Children were in before she got out of bed in the morning; Randy Lepper was often there as early as 9 a.m. Mrs. Wright, feeling nagged and tired, was losing her ironing, and she began to focus her resentment on Sylvia.

Things got worse in August, but there were still some happy times. Sylvia found things not a great deal worse than they had ever been for her. But the month was to be marked by two incidents, impugning her honesty and her chastity, which may have helped Gertrude rally resentment of the other children against Sylvia. The incidents involved Sylvia's admission of a sexual indiscretion in California earlier in the year, and an accusation of stealing.

But in Sylvia's mind, the incidents were obscured by the happier thoughts, like trips to the parks and the regular attendance at Sunday school with the Baniszewski children. They all attended the Memorial Baptist Church, a fundamentalist institution on Alabama Street near a bawdy movie house. When the movie house burned down later, the church's pastor, the Rev. Roy Julian, praised the fire as an "act of God" and "the answer to our prayers."

The Rev. Mr. Julian was pleased at the Likens girls' regular attendance at his church, and he was particularly proud of them on Sunday, August 22. That day, accompanied by the Baniszewski girls, Jenny and Sylvia "came forward" before the congregation and publicly confessed their faith.

But although Paula came forward too, her spirit seemed less than Christian. On the first of August she had broken her wrist slugging Sylvia on the jaw and then bragged about it at church. It was common knowledge in the congregation. Paula even told one church matron, "I tried to kill her."

The woman passed it off as so much childish talk.

Paula gave that impression—childishness, immaturity. She had managed to get through nine and a half years of school and was not stupid, but she made no strong effort to understand. She preferred to explain all happenings as acts of God.

Perhaps she was saddled with too much responsibility at too early an age. Playing second-in-command to an emotionally unstable adult was hardly good on-the-job training for adulthood. But Paula's physical appearance, with 160 pounds hanging on a 5-foot-4½-inch frame, did little to evoke any sympathy for her. And something had instilled a streak of meanness in her.

The fracture of her wrist did not stop her; the cast she wore for six weeks was just another weapon. She slammed Sylvia in the mouth with it, and blood spurted. Sylvia cried.

Paula was satisfied in her own mind that Sylvia had called Mrs. Wright an unspeakable name. "If you say anything else," she told Sylvia, "I'm going to break the cast on you." Paula had merely taken her mother's word for it that Sylvia had made the foul utterance; she had not heard any name-calling herself.

How many false charges were levied against Sylvia? No one will ever know. But she was "spanked" the day Mrs. Wright missed $10 from her purse, and Mrs. Wright told Sylvia she knew she was stealing from the neighborhood drug store, too.

If Sylvia ever had $10 during her stay with Mrs. Wright, no one saw her spend it. Had she any money, she surely would have spent it on food. She was always hungry. She was a growing girl, and she needed something to eat. But when she managed to find some nourishment the other children missed out on, she was punished.

The home's food supply was especially low the third week in August, a couple of days before Gertrude's child support check was due. The only milk in the house was reserved for the baby, Dennis Wright Jr. The rest of the family were down to soup and crackers, then only toast and margarine. The children had to eat their soup in shifts, because there were only three spoons in the house. Later, two of them were lost.

Envy reigned. If someone got something to eat, the others knew, and they were not happy about it. One Sunday, in the evening, the children received a rare treat: They attended a church supper. Sylvia had the first opportunity in weeks to eat something she liked. She would be sorry. When the children got home, Paula tattled on both Sylvia and Jenny for "eating too much." They were stripped, and they "got the board."

Sylvia was clubbed 15 times on the back.

One day the girls met their older sister, Dianna—a divorcee at 18—in the park. She bought Sylvia a sandwich. Sylvia thought she would get away with that one, but Marie Baniszewski remembered it two months later, and the punishment was worse than 15 blows on the back.

One time, Sylvia's "gluttony" was dealt with at a kitchen table session involving an adulterated hot dog. Gertrude's, Paula's and Randy Lepper's hot dogs were just like ball-park frankfurters, but Sylvia's had something extra. It was passed around the table so the others could take turns loading it with mustard, ketchup and other spices. When she was forced to eat it, she vomited. So they made her try it again. She would have preferred that second helping to something she was forced to eat late in October.

There also were times she didn't eat at all. One such day in September, Gertrude had given Jenny a quarter to spend at a school festival, and Jenny came home with a sucker. "Don't you wish you had one, Sylvia?" Gertrude taunted. Not too long afterward, Sylvia was given a bowl of soup, but was told to eat it with her fingers.

Another time Sylvia did not eat was when Gertrude was convinced she *had* eaten. "I smell White Castles on your breath," Gertrude said. "Danny bought you a hamburger, didn't he?" Gertrude also saw mustard on Sylvia's lips, but Jenny and the little children didn't.

Sylvia insisted she had not seen her brother Danny since school let out, and she certainly had not had a hamburger, such a sin as it was. But Gertrude was convinced and slugged Sylvia in the eye until it became black and blue, trying to make her confess. Whether or not Paula had seen mustard or smelled White Castle onions, she too was convinced that Sylvia deserved to be punished. She yanked at Sylvia's long tresses and pulled her from the kitchen chair onto the floor.

"I didn't," Sylvia sobbed, picking herself up. "I wasn't with him."

Jenny also bore the brunt of unjust punishment. One day at Brookside Park, she spotted an abandoned tennis shoe. Because of her deformity, she did not need shoes that matched, so she tried on the lone shoe and wore it home.

"Did you steal that?" Gertrude asked. Her children—Paula, Stephanie, Shirley, Marie and Jimmy—glared at Jenny tensely.

"No," the accused girl replied.

"Don't lie to me," Gertrude said. Her voice was heavy with menace.

"I'm not lying to you," Jenny pleaded.

"Paula, get the board," Gertrude instructed. Sylvia got about 10 licks then too because she had been at the park with Jenny and failed to confirm Mrs. Wright's suspicion.

Mr. and Mrs. Likens visited their daughters about the middle of August, but they saw nothing out of the way, and the girls did not complain, other than to say they were hungry and would like to go to a drive-in for a Coke or a hamburger. They were accustomed to being punished, often unjustly.

Gertrude's temper was not improved by getting involved with the wrong end of the law for the first time in her life, at the age of 37, in August. Her physical condition was such that she didn't feel like working;

the asthma season was just coming on. Paula was not working at the time either, and the support money was neither enough nor regular. Among the first to suffer in the vicious economic circle was the neighborhood newspaper boy. Mrs. Wright had not paid him; and that, in Indianapolis, is a crime. Police served a warrant on Mrs. Wright on August 18, 1965, for failure to pay a newsboy. When she also failed to answer the warrant, and police were sent to arrest her August 27, she became defiant.

Now she faced two charges—defrauding a newsboy and resisting arrest. She paid fines of $1 and costs on each count in Municipal Court the 29th of September. That was her total police record until October 26, 1965.

Things in general looked ominous for Sylvia, but she was buoyed by her confession of faith in church August 22. She told Gertrude she was "saved."

"Are you?" the woman asked.

"I don't think so," said Paula.

Sylvia had only a few more opportunities to get right with God. Most of the remaining Sunday mornings of her life she was kept home to get the house ready for company.

Lester Likens and his wife visited the Baniszewski home again August 26, and Lester gave Mrs. Wright another cash payment for boarding his daughters. Had he only known the double meaning of that word.

Lester eventually produced money order receipts to prove $220 was paid to Mrs. Wright over the three months his daughters stayed with her, and he testified he paid her at least $80 more in cash.

That the Baniszewski home was a neighborhood mecca is no wonder. A house full of girls is enough attraction for neighborhood boys. These included Richard Hobbs, Randy Lepper, Mike Monroe, Stephanie's boyfriend, Coy Hubbard, and others. Couple this attraction with Gertrude's fondness for boys, and the picture becomes clearer. Gertrude's paramour, Dennis Wright, was not yet of voting age when he fathered the 37-year-old woman's youngest child. Gertrude was still a woman, and she appreciated the boys' presence as much as Paula and Stephanie did. The boys liked her, too.

To show her appreciation, she danced for Richard Hobbs to phonograph music in the front room. To an adult male who had been to a night club even once in his life, the unsightly, scrawny woman's dancing might have been ludicrous. To a 14-year-old boy, it was at least a new experience, especially when her shoulder strap slipped off. If a 37-year-old woman is drawn to teenage boys, it follows that teenage girls are her rivals.

Mrs. Wright and the Likens girls began talking about sex the latter part of August. Sylvia was reminiscing on her happy days in Long Beach, and she longed for her California boyfriend. Mrs. Wright began asking questions.

"Have you ever done anything with a boy, Sylvia?" she got around to asking.

"I guess so," Sylvia said, not sure just what Mrs. Wright meant. She talked about the times she went skating with the boys and she and Jenny went with boys to a park on the beach.

Jenny and Stephanie joined the conversation. The talk drifted to a party the Likens children gave for their friends the time their parents took a two-day trip to Las Vegas. Sylvia admitted that she had crawled under the covers with her boyfriend.

"Why did you do that, Sylvia?" Mrs. Wright asked.

"I don't know," the girl said, shrugging.

Several days later, Mrs. Wright reminded the girl of her indiscretion. "You're certainly getting big in the stomach, Sylvia," she said. "It looks like you're going to have a baby."

Sylvia thought she was being kidded. "Yeah, it sure is getting big," she agreed. "I'm just going to have to go on a diet."

But Mrs. Wright was not kidding. She assured Sylvia and her own girls that any time they "did something" with a boy, they were sure to have a baby. And she kicked Sylvia between the legs to emphasize her point.

Paula was scandalized by Sylvia's admission of indiscretion. Knocking Sylvia from her chair to the kitchen floor, she scolded, "You ain't fit to sit in a chair." Had that fat, rejected girl forgotten her own indiscretion with her Kentucky lover? Events proved, at any rate, that Paula was pregnant, and Sylvia was not.

Gertrude returned often to the sex theme. Was she madly jealous of Sylvia's sex appeal? Was *she* responsible for the vicious mauling of the girl's pubic region that showed up in the autopsy?

4

SCHOOL DAYS

THE ROLLING campus of Arsenal Technical High School is nearly a half-mile long and a quarter-mile deep. Situated on an old military campsite, Tech occupies many buildings and boasts more than 4,000 pupils. It is the largest preparatory school in the state of Indiana. It annually graduates more pupils from its night division than most high schools graduate in total. Within the iron rail fences enclosing the green grounds are a gymnasium and football stadium, academic buildings, an industrial shop and other facilities.

The size of the place, the iron fence and the austere brick buildings cause many a passerby to confuse Tech with the Indiana Women's Prison. Tech is further west, in a slightly nicer neighborhood, but many of the inmates are just as tough. In the fall of 1965 they included Paula Baniszewski, Stephanie Baniszewski, and—Sylvia Marie Likens.

Tech is bordered on the west by Oriental Street and on the east by the antique neighborhood Woodruff Place. The address is 1500 East Michigan Street. That places it two blocks north and two miles, three blocks west of 3850 East New York Street, where two pretty teenage girls with lovely long hair set out nervously for the first day of school early in September 1965.

Stephanie Baniszewski loved school. At a habeas corpus hearing four months later, when she was trying to get out of jail and back into school, she told a judge, "If school were a man, I'd marry it." Her brothers and sisters called her "Einy" (for Einstein) because she brought home A's and B's on her report cards. Her narrow, plastic-framed glasses gave her radiant face an intelligent look.

Stephanie wanted to be a lawyer. Whenever her mother visited her lawyer, in hopes of dragging some more support money out of one of her ex-husbands, Stephanie went along. But Stephanie was not studying law at this time, nor did she have any idea she would soon have a need for legal advice. She was at present concerned with English and biology.

Her companion was Sylvia Likens, who by this time had become her good friend. At home they sang to one another. Stephanie would sing her favorite song to Sylvia, and Sylvia would reciprocate. Sylvia's favorite was Shirley Bassey's "Reach for the Stars." She looked upward with hopes and dreams.

Sylvia did not share Stephanie's love for school; she had been enrolled in Tech before and had dropped out on her 16th birthday. But she had a good reason for going back. Both she and Stephanie had jobs in the school cafeteria, and that meant a free hot lunch every day, something they did not get at home.

The Baniszewskis lived on the borderline of the Tech district. Richard Hobbs, who lived just around the corner, went to Thomas Carr Howe High School, a mile to the east. Stephanie's boyfriend also went to Howe, where he was a troublemaker. Six feet tall and carrying 170 pounds, Coy Hubbard had found at the age of 15 that he did not have to take any lip from anybody, and that included teachers.

Sylvia had no reason to fear Coy at that time; in fact, he was one of her friends. She had met him before school started, had accompanied Stephanie to Coy's house on Linwood Avenue twice. In turn, Stephanie had accompanied Jenny and Sylvia to visit their Grandmother Grimes, who lived not far away.

Paula also re-entered Tech that fall, as a sophomore in the evening division. She worked at a drug store in the daytime.

Johnny Baniszewski, who had been living with his father, also returned to his mother's home that September so that he could resume his education at Public School No. 78, where the other Baniszewski children and Jenny Likens were enrolled. Johnny, at 12 years, was large for his age. His straight brown hair drooped slightly over his forehead, and he showed signs of becoming a handsome young man. His quick, round eyes gave him an impish look.

When Lester Likens visited his daughters the last

day of September, he was pleased to learn that both were back in school. He was confident he had done the right thing in leaving them with Mrs. Wright. Had he checked with the Tech High School administration, he would have seen a different picture. Sylvia's attendance record was spotty. Her last day there was October 6, one day after Mr. and Mrs. Likens' last visit to the Baniszewski home.

In a school so large as Tech, one would think that one quiet, retiring girl might not be missed. That is not true. The school sent repeated notices to Mrs. Wright inquiring about Sylvia's absences. Mrs. Wright answered some of the notices and even made visits to the schools to talk to Sylvia and Jenny's teachers. The teachers, impressed by the woman's apparent concern for the girls, were saddened to learn they had no great interest in school.

Even Stephanie was surprised at Sylvia's poor attendance. She was puzzled when Sylvia eventually dropped out altogether. "She just doesn't want to go," Stephanie's mother told her.

That may have been true, notwithstanding the fact that Mrs. Wright had forbidden her to go. Sylvia had enough unhappy experiences at Tech High School to want to stay home.

One involved a remark she had made to a male classmate.

A stranger approached Stephanie in the hall at Tech one day to ask how much she took.

"What are you talking about?" Stephanie demanded.

"How much do you want to go to bed with me?" the boy specified.

"Who told you I'd do that?" Stephanie was indignant. She may have been the only virgin in the Baniszewski household.

"A friend of yours," the boy laughed.

"Some friend," Stephanie snorted.

"Her name is Sylvia," the boy told her.

When Stephanie got home, she had it out with Sylvia. When Sylvia admitted planting the rumor, Stephanie slugged her in the chin. Sylvia, in tears, apologized. That brought tears to Stephanie's eyes too. But it did not end there.

Sylvia, smarting from all the chiding she had suffered in regard to her own sexual experience, had spread rumors about Paula too. Johnny brought one of the rumors home.

When Coy Hubbard heard about the aspersions on his beloved's purity, he flew into a rage. He slapped Sylvia, banged her head against the wall and gave her a flip, judo style, onto her back on the floor. He never forgave her.

Neither did Mrs. Wright. She gave Sylvia the board at the time, and grosser indignities were to follow.

But the incident that served as Mrs. Wright's pretense for keeping Sylvia out of school was the alleged theft of another girl's gym suit.

Sylvia needed a suit for her physical education class. One morning, before setting out for school, she asked Mrs. Wright for money to buy one, and was refused. When she came home that evening, she had a gym suit.

"I bet she took it," Gertrude mumbled to her children. Stephanie had not gone to school with Sylvia that day and could not help her. She lay half asleep in the front room, recovering from a poisonous spider bite that had kept her out of school for two days. She dozed off again but was soon awakened by loud bickering between Gertrude and Sylvia.

"You took it!" Gertrude accused.

"No," Sylvia pleaded. "I found it, on the sidewalk."

Gertrude slapped her on the face and arms and kicked her shins. "You took it!" she shouted, tousling Sylvia's hair roughly.

"All right," Sylvia cried, "I took it!" That was a mistake. The confession in, the punishment began. Sylvia was whipped with a three-inch-wide black police belt, which John Baniszewski Sr. had given his ex-wife a couple of years before to apply to their children when they got out of order. Mrs. Wright, remembering a mysteriously acquired tennis shoe, whipped Jenny too.

Then she sat Sylvia on the couch and began lecturing her again on the evils of premarital sex. Sylvia did not realize that "Mrs. Wright" had never been married to "Mr. Wright," who had gotten her pregnant twice.

"You should never do anything with a boy until you're married," the woman lectured.

"I didn't," Sylvia whined.

Mrs. Wright kicked her in the vagina. "You should never, never, never, never, never . . . ," she repeated. Sylvia moaned. Stephanie jumped out of bed, screaming at her mother. "She didn't do anything!"

Stephanie was crying when Coy Hubbard came over, and Mrs. Wright explained to him that Sylvia had upset her. So he helped the woman apply her macabre discipline.

To impress upon Sylvia the sin of sticky fingers, for stealing a gym suit, Mrs. Wright held a lighted match to Sylvia's fingers. "I don't want to ever catch you stealing anything again," she said.

"I hate you!" the woman shouted, whipping Sylvia in the rear three times more. "You're ruining my life!"

She told Sylvia and Jenny both, "Get your clothes. You're going to the Juvenile Center." She did not follow through on that threat, and, as justice would have it, it was her own children who wound up at the center for delinquents, within six weeks.

5

MOB PSYCHOLOGY

GERTRUDE WRIGHT had a sense of timing that could turn child's play into sadism. A psychologically passive woman among her peers, she had a way with children—an evil way. For whatever motive, she was able to mobilize children's play energy to serve her own dark purposes with Sylvia Likens. In this sordid venture, she was ably seconded by her aide-de-camp, Paula, who had become extremely jealous of Sylvia.

What started as horseplay turned out to be quite rough on the wretched Likens girl. One popular household sport at 3850 East New York Street in the autumn of 1965 was judo. The children practiced judo flips on one another; the mattress on the floor provided a handy landing mat.

Paula, Stephanie, Coy and Sylvia were playing the game one day; and when Coy flipped Sylvia, he missed the mattress. That was fun, and it set the pattern from then on. Coy later found the judo flip to be an effective form of punishment when he believed Sylvia had questioned Stephanie's virtue.

Sylvia was a flipper too, but she always managed to come out on the short end of things. For example, there was the day Jimmy leaped on her back for a promised piggy-back ride. Sylvia, surprised, exercised her new skill to flip the boy on the floor. But Jimmy had kidney trouble, and his sister Shirley naturally thought it mean to toss him on his back. She slapped Sylvia. Sylvia did not slap back. Mrs. Wright and the children learned to take advantage of her reluctance to fight back.

Pudgy, whiny-voiced Anna Siscoe, 13, found herself in a fight with Sylvia the first of September. When it was all over, she realized it was Mrs. Wright who had caused the fight and encouraged it.

Anna originally liked Sylvia, as did nearly all those who knew her. But she did not appreciate the remarks Sylvia was supposed to have made about her mother. Mrs. Wright told the Siscoe girl, "Sylvia said your mother goes out with all sorts of men for $5." Anna slapped and kicked the unresisting Sylvia, then dug in her fingernails and scraped the length of Sylvia's back.

Other children moved to break up the fight, but Mrs. Wright called out, "Let them fight their own fight. Get up, Sylvia." The girl kicked Sylvia in the abdomen; Sylvia writhed and clutched her belly, moaning, "Oh, my baby!" It appeared that Mrs. Wright had convinced her she was pregnant. After the fight, Mrs. Wright graciously applied Merthiolate to Sylvia's wounds.

Fights with Judy Duke and Paula and Stephanie

had similar origin and encouragement. A pretty 12-year-old blonde with a lagging I.Q., Judy slapped and kicked Sylvia when told by Mrs. Wright that Sylvia had called her a bitch.

Paula was choking Sylvia once in September. Gertrude pulled her daughter off twice, then assumed an air of indifference. "Just let them fight; it's their fight," she said. Paula had been told that Sylvia had spread rumors she was a whore.

Sylvia's supposedly best friend in the house, Stephanie, also went along with the rumor-fed mob psychology. Told by just about everyone that Sylvia had been bad, Stephanie took it upon herself to apply the paddle.

Before long, the mob psychology had turned it into a game. Paula would club Sylvia in the head with whatever she could find—hair-spray cans, dishes, bottles; as soon as Stephanie would grab one weapon away, Paula would grab another one. One evening at dinner, Paula tossed a soft drink bottle across the table, striking Sylvia in the hand.

Gertrude's aim was more accurate. Upstairs, she plunked Sylvia in the head with a bottle. Although Gertrude's special talent was in egging children into bullying Sylvia, she was not above grappling with the girl herself. She doubled her fists like a boxer, and punched the girl repeatedly. Sylvia dared not fight back.

One of Gertrude's complaints against Sylvia was $35 in medical bills. It was the "problems with Sylvia" that were causing her asthma and nervous anxiety, and some hyperventilation blackouts that Stephanie was suffering at the time, she reasoned.

Since what the neighborhood children believed was generally what Gertrude had told them (she was their friend, just one of the girls), and Sylvia never asserted herself enough to tell her own side of the story, the children generally sided with Gertrude against Sylvia. A game developed in which, at one time, more than ten children participated in beating, kicking and flipping Sylvia and burning her with matches or cigarettes. Johnny Baniszewski and Randy Lepper took turns punching her in the face. Even Jenny was forced into the act. "Get over and slap your sister," Gertrude ordered. Jenny hesitated; so Gertrude slapped *her* on the face. Jenny slapped Sylvia's cheek, using her left hand in an effort not to hurt her.

Once when Judy Duke slapped Sylvia, having been informed that Sylvia had called her a bitch, Shirley Baniszewski ripped open Sylvia's blouse. Richard Hobbs wandered into the kitchen, remarking, "Everybody's having fun with Sylvia." That was when Anna Siscoe "had fun" stomping and clawing Sylvia, kicking her in the stomach. When Sylvia cried, "Oh, my baby!" it was more than Judy could take. She went home sick.

Mrs. Wright was not sick, but she did call a living room conference of the children on October 1 to announce, "We're all going to have to learn to get along better." Sylvia and her friend Darlene McGuire were there. "My girls and I have plans, Sylvia," Gertrude explained, "and we don't want you to interrupt them."

Paula had her own solution. The middle of September, she had taken Sylvia to the back door, saying, "Get away and stay away. Get out for your own safety." Sylvia did not know where to go; this was the only home she knew at the time. She stayed.

A few days after Gertrude's living room conference, Sylvia and Jenny's parents came to visit them before leaving with the carnival for Florida. Mr. Likens gave Mrs. Wright another $20, and he gave Sylvia some money for shoes. He and his wife had brought both Jenny and Sylvia some school clothes.

The girls mentioned that they were hungry. Reports had been circulating the neighborhood that Sylvia had been seen eating out of garbage cans. The girls' parents took them out for a Coke.

Likens told Mrs. Wright he was due back in three weeks; it was then October 5, 1965. The next day would be Sylvia's last at Tech High School. Two and a half weeks later, Mrs. Wright would receive the last concerned notice from the school administrators, asking whether there was anything they could do to help. Three weeks to the day after the Likenses' last visit—on October 26—their daughter would die.

NO MORE than four feet from the Baniszewskis' back door stood another frame house, owned by the same real estate company and rented at the same price, $55 a month. All the rentals along New York

Street were packed closely together. The inhabitants were a restless lot, moving in and out frequently. The houses were run-down, dirty, and in need of paint. It could not be classified a slum area, but it did not make the grade of "middle class" either. No one was particularly happy to be living there.

Into the house next door, at 3848 East New York, moved Mr. and Mrs. Raymond Vermillion and their two children around the end of August. A couple approaching middle age, Vermillion and his wife, Phyllis, had hoped for something more middle class. But it was a home.

Mrs. Vermillion, a rather attractive woman in earlier years, worked on the night shift at the huge Radio Corporation of America plant on Sherman Drive, not far away. One of her first chores in the new location was to find someone to care for her children. Shortly after breakfast the first day she was settled, she called on her next-door neighbor, Mrs. Gertrude Wright.

Gertrude was in no mood for company but wanted to be neighborly. When she heard the rap on the door, she asked her new neighbor to come in.

Most of the children were home. The clamor Mrs. Vermillion encountered soon convinced her that this was no place to leave her children, aged 6 and 1½. The older children in the Baniszewski house were shouting at each other and banging around. The baby, Dennis, screamed and jumped at each sound.

But the woman found that she liked Mrs. Wright and felt a great deal of empathy for her too. Mrs.

Vermillion knew it could be trying just to take care of two children, and she felt for any woman saddled with the responsibility of nine. She and Mrs. Wright were not far apart in age, but Gertrude looked old enough to be Mrs. Vermillion's mother.

"Yes," Gertrude told her, "these children get on my nerves at times. I had to run the neighbor kids out of the house this morning." But she said she believed she could take on two more for $10 a week. "Just as long as I only keep them while you work; that shouldn't be too much trouble," Gertrude said.

Mrs. Vermillion was not sure she wanted to leave her children here at this time, and she wanted to get better acquainted. So when Gertrude offered her a cup of coffee, she accepted. Mrs. Wright sighed and instructed Paula to bring Mrs. Vermillion a cup of coffee.

Glancing toward the kitchen, the neighbor woman took note of some of the children. Besides Paula, she saw two boys, whom she later learned were Paula's and Stephanie's boyfriends. Then her sharp eyes were drawn to a slender young girl sitting at the dining room table.

"Why, child," she asked, "how did you get the black eye?"

Sylvia turned her head away without speaking.

"Get out of my sight," Gertrude shouted. "Get into the kitchen, Sylvia. I don't want nothing to do with you. Go on. I hate you."

Mrs. Wright heaved another sigh and regained her composure. "That's Sylvia," she said. "Her parents

are with some carnival. She's three months pregnant. I just don't know what I am going to do with
her."

Paula knew what to do with her as soon as Sylvia
got into the kitchen. She filled a tumbler at the hot
water spigot and tossed the contents into the girl's
face. Sylvia shrieked in pain. Paula then applied some
margarine to the scalded area. Mrs. Vermillion tried
not to watch the proceedings, but it was difficult.

As Paula brought the coffee she boasted noncha-
lantly, "*I* gave her the black eye."

"Get on up to your room, Sylvia!" Mrs. Wright
ordered. As the girl reached the top of the stairs, the
woman added, "If you're pregnant, I'm going to kill
you!"

Gertrude shook her head. "She hasn't had a period in three months," she told her new neighbor.

Mrs. Vermillion made other arrangements for her
children, but she maintained a social acquaintance
with Gertrude. She stopped over again in October
for a cup of coffee after breakfast. The Baniszewski
children were just finishing a breakfast of toast and
jelly.

Sylvia came into the room, and Mrs. Vermillion
noticed that she had another black eye, and that her
mouth was swollen.

"I beat her up again," Paula volunteered. "She's
nothing but trouble."

Mrs. Vermillion fidgeted. She knew Paula was
attending night school, but she wondered what Sylvia was doing home.

"I had to make her quit school," Gertrude explained. "She stole a gym suit there. Then she stole a watch from down the street. Can you imagine? I don't know how I'm going to pay those people back. I guess I'll just have to take some out of Sylvia's ironing money."

Sylvia seemed to be in a daze. Frightened and nervous the first time Mrs. Vermillion saw her, she now looked as though she didn't care about anything. Soon, Paula began shouting something at her; Mrs. Vermillion could not make out all the words. But she saw Paula pick up a thick black belt and crack it on Sylvia's flesh.

"MOMMY," THE high-voiced girl was telling her mother, "they were over there beating and fighting with her. They were beating and kicking Sylvia something terrible."

Mrs. Duke, a pretty brunette, was busy washing the dishes. "Oh, well, Judy," she sighed. "They're just punishing her, aren't they?"

"Yes," the girl said. She hesitated. "I guess."

Mrs. Duke had not met Mrs. Wright, but she had heard nothing really derogatory about her. She knew Judy got things mixed up once in a while, and she knew every child's capacity for exaggeration. Besides, a woman might be expected to fly off the handle at a child's misbehavior if she had nine children to look after.

Other neighbors had been inside the Baniszewski home, and they reported nothing abnormal, except for the wild carryings on that would be expected in a household with nine children. The lady from the other half of the double once complained of the constant noise. Neighbors as far as four doors away were to tell police later that they heard screams coming from somewhere but did not think much about it.

Mike Monroe's mother had visited the house. So had Randy Lepper's mother. Darlene McGuire's father had come over to the house once in the summer, but he did not go inside. Most of them felt sorry for Mrs. Wright, a poor, sick, hard-working mother with all those kids to take care of.

THE REV. Roy Julian visited Mrs. Wright in September to talk over her problems with her. Julian was fairly young, and decidedly handsome, and he spoke with a clipped, precise voice that resounded with Godliness.

The dynamic preacher made it a point to visit all the members of his congregation regularly, to talk with them, to try to bring them closer to the Lord, if possible. He was particularly concerned about Mrs. Wright, who seldom attended church, although he knew she must be tired on Sunday mornings, as well as all the other times. But the Rev. Mr. Julian was also concerned because of some of the things Paula had said; surely a girl in a Christian home could not break her wrist on another girl's jaw and feel good about it.

"Good afternoon, Mrs. Wright," said the sandy-haired minister as she let him in the door. "How are you today?" He managed to smile cheerfully.

Gertrude grasped at the offer of sympathy. "Oh, I don't feel so good," she said. "Sometimes I can hardly catch my breath." She coughed. "I've been taking this medicine the doctor gave me," she sighed, "but it seems to affect me about as bad as the bronchitis in a different way. It really dopes me up. I have to spend half my time in bed. And the kids!—they're just running wild.

"I'm not able to stay up a full day, but I try to take in some ironing. My husband don't pay the support like he should. I'm trying to keep the family going with the ironing, but the customers are getting pretty impatient."

The minister sympathized, but had no concrete advice to offer her. They prayed as they sat together on the couch.

"The children—mostly Sylvia—are causing me quite a few problems," Mrs. Wright continued. "They're giving me quite a case of nerves. I take medicine for that too. Dr. Lindenborg gave me some phenobarbital.

"I started to correct the children. I tried to spank Sylvia once, but I couldn't because of my asthma. Paula had to help me.

"Sylvia has been skipping school," she told the preacher, "and making advances on some older men, for money. I had to lock her in her room upstairs because she would slip out at night."

Julian prayed with her again, and he wanted also

to have a talk with Sylvia. But Jenny had been sitting through their conference, and Gertrude said, "Here's her sister; you can ask her."

"What about your sister, child?" Julian asked.

"She tells lies," Jenny responded quietly. "And at night, after all of us go to bed, she slips down and raids the icebox."

"She took the baby's milk once," Gertrude said.

Julian left the home with a heavy heart. He came back a few weeks later, after Paula told him the family was worried about Stephanie, who had been suffering blackouts again. The doctor had not been able to explain it, and there had been some worry about a brain tumor.

But Mrs. Wright was still dwelling on her problems with Sylvia. The minister wrung his hands in despair, and they prayed again.

"Sylvia said at school," Mrs. Wright said, "that Paula was going to have a baby. But I know my daughter, and I know Sylvia. Paula's not going to have a baby; it's Sylvia."

"Paula told me," the minister said, "that there was some hatred in her heart for Sylvia." Mrs. Wright assured him that Paula was just trying to help her manage the house, that Sylvia was the only one who was hateful.

The Rev. Mr. Julian left the house for the last time; he was never again to see Sylvia, his eager Sunday school pupil. The next time he was to face Mrs. Wright was in court, from the witness stand.

Mrs. Wright had another visitor, the 15th day of

October, 1965, and she handled her with the calmness of a cunning criminal.

The young, white-uniformed woman rapped on the door in the middle of the afternoon. "Come in," bade Mrs. Wright, puzzled.

"Mrs. Wright?" the woman said in a pleasant, professional tone. "I'm Mrs. Sanders, a public health nurse. How are you?" She glanced about the room; Jenny sat in a corner. The nurse recognized her from seeing her at Public School 78. They nodded greetings at one another.

"I've come to talk to you about your children," the nurse explained, trying to make it appear to be a routine visit. Mrs. Wright held the baby, Dennis; Paula also was in the room.

The conversation ranged from general hygiene to diet. Then the pretty nurse asked, "Are any of your children ill, Mrs. Wright?"

"No, they haven't been," the woman replied, somewhat indignant.

"Well," the nurse continued, "we received an anonymous phone call that there were children here with open, running sores."

"You can check my children," Mrs. Wright said. "None of them have open sores on their body."

"Well, this woman said there was one girl with sores all over her body," the nurse continued. Jenny sat staring, motionless, her eyes wide open.

Gertrude bristled. "Jenny, go do the dishes!" she snapped. Calmed down some, she said firmly, "I know who you're looking for. Jenny's sister, Sylvia.

She has sores all over her body; she won't keep herself clean. I finally kicked her out of the house." Mrs. Sanders wanted to know why.

"She's not worthy to stay here," Mrs. Wright said. "She's a prostitute; she runs around with all the neighborhood boys." Paula chimed in with her own distaste for Sylvia.

"I don't know where she would be now," Gertrude said. Jenny knew that her sister was then in the basement of that very house, but she did not say anything. Gertrude and Paula knew it, too.

"She even called my daughters prostitutes," Gertrude said, continuing the verbal barrage. "Who called you, anyway?"

"I don't know," the nurse said. "I didn't take the call. It was an anonymous call." She later was to learn that the caller was Mike Monroe's mother, from a few doors down the street.

Mrs. Sanders rose to leave. She drove to her office and filed a report on a "one time only" card.

Other visitors to the home that fall included the police. Besides the two runs they made to 3850 East New York Street in connection with Mrs. Wright's failure to pay the newsboy, they made runs to the house on September 10 and October 20, 1965. The September 10 run was for first aid for Marie Baniszewski, who had accidentally cut a gash in her wrist. Police rushed her to Community Hospital for stitches to close the wound.

The October 20 run was on a report of a burglary. The youth who lived in the other half of the house,

Robert Bruce Hanlon, banged on the door that evening, demanding the return of some things he said the children had stolen from his basement.

Gertrude told him be was knocking at the wrong door, and they argued on the porch. She called the police, telling them she had found Hanlon halfway through her window. The police locked him up on a burglary charge.

Mrs. Vermillion and her husband had witnessed practically the whole scene from their car, parked in the street. When Mrs. Vermillion heard the youth could get a 10-to-20-year sentence for burglary, she became concerned. As a witness, she helped free him of the charge.

Jenny saw her older sister, Dianna Shoemaker, in the park twice in September, but no one was too concerned about Sylvia then. When Jenny did become concerned, she was too frightened to tell anyone.

6

NO FRIENDS IN NEED

LITTLE JENNY Likens was confused. Staring her in the face, from the top of her wooden desk in her eighth grade general science class, was something she understood to be a "tuition." Gertrude had told her never to bring a "tuition" home with her "because I won't pay it." But the teacher had told Jenny, as she understood it, that since her parents did not own any house or furniture, she would have to pay tuition. It was $165. She could not take it home to Gertrude, and the teacher would not let her go home without it.

"Maybe I should take it to Grandmother Grimes," thought Jenny. "She doesn't live too far away, down near Southeastern Avenue. I could probably get there before suppertime. But if Gertrude found out, I'd get the belt. And if I don't get home right after school, Sylvia will get the belt. I'd hate to leave Sylvia alone there. I wish Sylvia were with me now so we could both go to Grandmother Grimes.

"Sylvia was always so good to me," Jenny's

thoughts continued. "I remember the times she took me to Rollerland. She knew I couldn't skate, so she made me put a skate on my good foot, and she gave me her hand and pulled me around the rink. Sylvia was so nice to me. I just couldn't go to Grandmother Grimes and leave her alone at Gertrude's. Something awful might happen. But I can't take the tuition home. Gertrude'll hit the ceiling. I'll get the belt, or the board. Oh, what'll I do!"

She took the "tuition" home. Gertrude's reaction was not so violent as expected. She just laid the "tuition" on a high shelf and said she would give it to Sylvia and Jenny's daddy.

Lester Likens never paid the tuition. As events proved, his daughters never got their full year of school anyway.

The last time Jenny and Sylvia had seen their older sister Dianna in the park was a hot, still day in September. The smell of autumn had not yet pervaded the air. They told Dianna that Sylvia had it pretty rough. Every time something went wrong, they said, it was "Paula, get the board!"

But Dianna thought they were exaggerating. Their own father had used a belt himself to keep his girls in line, and usually they deserved it. Once in California, Sylvia and Danny had gotten it for staying out all night. Back in Indianapolis, Sylvia and Jenny got it for fooling around in the supermarket when they should have been on their way home. Dianna had felt that sting of leather herself. So she didn't pay much attention, even though Sylvia and Jenny insisted that Sylvia was getting it for things she had not done.

Sylvia did not see Dianna again. She and Jenny were not sure where Dianna lived. They saw her in the park a lot, and they thought she lived on Tuxedo Street or Sherman Drive or around in there. But she moved around a lot. The police found her for Jenny the night of October 26 so that Jenny would have a place to spend the night.

In the house, Sylvia and Jenny liked Stephanie and Shirley the best. Both of them were friendly and "real nice girls," Jenny thought. They were not really mean like the others. Like Johnny, for instance. She thought of the one time after school when he slipped up behind her sister, shouted "Hey, Sylvia!" and punched her on the arm when she wheeled around, saying, "That's for calling my mother a name." No one, not even Johnny, had actually heard Sylvia calling Gertrude a name, but Gertrude *said* Sylvia did.

Stephanie was upset. Her nervous fainting spells were cropping up again. After one hectic day, she sat down at the table, whipped off her glasses, and just cried. "Fighting, fighting!" she sobbed. "That's all we ever do around here! I wish we'd quit!"

One reason Stephanie felt so bad about it was because she had been in on it. She was thinking about the time Sylvia had come home from school and Gertrude ripped Sylvia's blouse off her to show Stephanie she was wearing Stephanie's brassiere. That made Stephanie mad. She pummeled Sylvia seven or eight times, repeating, "What do you want to do that for, Sylvia, why do you do it?" Sylvia just stood there, took it, and cried.

Stephanie was angriest the time she came home from school to find Sylvia nude in the middle of the living room, surrounded by a ring of onlookers including Randy Lepper, Johnny, Gertrude, Jenny and Paula. Sylvia was squatting, with a Pepsi bottle inserted in her vagina. Stephanie rushed to the middle of the room and slapped Sylvia, hard. "Get up to your room, Sylvia," she ordered.

She had not seen the prelude. She had not seen Gertrude order Sylvia to undress, and to spread her legs, and to insert the bottle, to prove to Jenny "what kind of girl you are."

Gertrude and Paula were most jealous of Sylvia. Gertrude often told Sylvia, "I could pass for 20. I could put my fancy clothes on, and saunter down the street, and get the boys to whistle and honk at me just like you do, Sylvia." But she knew it was not the truth. She had managed to convince the girls she was only 31, but she was not pretty. Thirteen pregnancies and a lifetime of hard work had taken care of her. The only boys she could attract were young boys who wanted the sexual experience, like Dennis Wright, who had planted his seed in her twice but then had beaten her and finally left her, and like Richard Hobbs, who was drawn to the home to watch Gertrude expose part of her belly as she danced to the striptease music from the phonograph, exulting, "This is just the way they do it down at the Fox Theater."

Paula had equal reason to be jealous. She knew she was pregnant, or at least had a good idea that she was. Despite the talk of Sylvia's pregnancy, Sylvia did not look pregnant. The autopsy was later to prove Sylvia was not. It was not fair that Sylvia was not pregnant; she was already prettier than Paula, wasn't that enough?

Stephanie had less reason to be jealous. She was slender, like Sylvia, and she was pretty too. She had a steady boyfriend, Coy Hubbard, who said he had loved her always. She also made good grades at school; she continually brought home A's and B's on her report card, and the other children enviously called her "Einy."

So Stephanie was able to accept Sylvia as a friend, striking out only when convinced—usually by Gertrude—that Sylvia had transgressed some moral precept, or when she saw Sylvia engaged in such revolting behavior as the Pepsi bottle incident. Of course, Stephanie had no idea of what was really going on; looking back, she could see that she herself might have been the target of the seething frustration that pervaded every corner of her home, had Sylvia not been there. But she could not see that at this time, and so her help for her friend Sylvia—when it came—was too little and too late.

7

CINDERELLA WITHOUT A PRINCE

WHAT SOCIOLOGICAL explanation could there be for the bizarre events that followed Sylvia Likens' last day of school, October 5, 1965? What strange comment was it on our civilization, the steady crescendo of events that led to a pretty girl's death in a crowded city neighborhood at the hands of a mob of children directed by a physically mature but grotesquely vengeful adult? What kind of jungle was the packed little neighborhood on East New York Street?

Readers of fairy tales, devotees of melodrama, might have seen some hope radiating from the Cinderella situation into which Sylvia was descending. The prime elements of the classic fairy tale were there: Sylvia was prettier than Mrs. Wright's true daughter Paula, but subordinated to her. Soon she found her new bed was a pile of rags in the basement. Extrapolating the situation in terms of the fairy tale, the devotees of melodrama could see an imminent rescue for Sylvia. But this was not melodrama. This was real life. Sylvia had no fairy godmother, and her prince never appeared.

It was about October 12, or two weeks before her death, that Sylvia intermittently began to share the basement with the puppy that was kept there. The reasoning was that Sylvia was not keeping herself clean—there was some talk she had wet the bed and therefore she did not deserve to sleep upstairs with the human beings. A visit to the doctor might have shown that Sylvia's incontinence was due to an injury to the kidneys, perhaps suffered in one of those judo flips in which Coy Hubbard missed the mattress. But the doctor money was reserved for Gertrude, who was suffering more frequent attacks of asthma and nerves brought on, she said, by her problems with Sylvia.

It was a typical basement, small and dank. Rickety wooden steps led to the bottom, turning 90 degrees to the left two steps down from the kitchen, then 90 degrees right, again two steps further down. The long flight the rest of the way down ended only a couple of feet short of the concrete east wall. Around to the left were a couple of sinks; a bare light bulb burned above. A partially clothed set of bed springs was stacked in the corner, but it was far beyond use. Sylvia's makeshift bed was a pile of rags and old clothes, halfway under the staircase, short of the large coal furnace.

The girl's descent to her dungeon was ceremonious. "Here's how you do it," Gertrude instructed Paula, Stephanie, Johnny, Randy Lepper and Coy

Hubbard. With that she gave Sylvia a shove, and she tumbled through the two 90-degree turns to the bottom. Coy Hubbard learned the lesson well, and soon improvised a variation. He gripped Sylvia's hands tightly behind her and gave her a quick start with his foot.

Paula also invented some variations. Descending from the second floor, where she had been to the bathroom, Sylvia was met on the stairs by Paula's outstretched foot, and tumbled into the living room. She was met at the bottom by Gertrude. "I hate you! I hate you!" Gertrude would shout. "You're going to get the hell out of my house!"

Sylvia's diet during her stay in the basement consisted largely of crackers and water, often only the former.

It was about the same time that the baths began. Still "concerned" about Sylvia's cleanliness, Gertrude arranged for her children to bathe her about every other night. They said Sylvia was reluctant to bathe, and no wonder: The tub was filled entirely from the hot water spigot.

To overcome Sylvia's reluctance, Gertrude or the children would bind her hands and feet and lift her into the tub. When she fainted in one of the baths, Gertrude yanked her hair and beat her head against the side of the tub to revive her. When Sylvia screamed, she was hit in the side of the head with the fraternity paddle. Eventually, Johnny tied gags in her mouth to keep her screams from disturbing the neighbors.

It was also about this time that Sylvia began her career as a human ashtray. Perhaps enticed by the smell of burning flesh the time she burned Sylvia's fingers for stealing, and remembering the time Dennis Wright put a cigarette out on her own neck, Gertrude tried the same trick on Sylvia. Sometimes she was content to toss lighted matches at the girl. One of them set her clothing on fire, but it was quickly extinguished.

The children soon picked up the smoker's habit, and Sylvia's body began to show the little round sores that Dr. Kebel found so many of when he examined her body.

There were also some big round sores, more the size of a baseball, and caused by something besides cigarettes. These larger sores received medical treatment. For instance, Gertrude applied rubbing alcohol to Sylvia's arms and legs. Jenny hoped this indicated the woman had some concern for her sister, after all.

Paula applied her own brand of first aid to the large raw spot on Sylvia's knee. Gertrude supplied the salt as Coy Hubbard held the patient. Paula rubbed a little in slowly. Hubbard said, "That ain't the way to do it," and they rubbed more in, hard. It just increased the bleeding and Sylvia screamed more.

Then there was the open sore Gertrude found in Sylvia's scalp. Her treatment for that was holding the girl's head under a faucet spouting scalding hot water.

Again, Paula had another method of dealing with the scalp problem. As Sylvia sat at the kitchen table one day, Paula just picked up a pair of scissors and snipped off Sylvia's prided long hair. "How do you like that?" Paula asked. Sylvia didn't, but she tried to agree she needed a haircut, and she asked for a lock as a souvenir. She didn't get it.

Paula had lost her job at the drug store. The management did not think she was "mature enough" to handle the job. But she was mature enough to assume a greater and greater degree of responsibility at home, as Gertrude was going farther and farther out of consciousness on her phenobarbital, antihistamine and Coricidin.

Paula also took over more and more of the discipline. She administered about 25 paddlings to Sylvia in her final two weeks, applying most of the blows to Sylvia's posterior.

Meanwhile, Coy Hubbard was getting in more judo practice. He flipped Sylvia over his shoulders, hard onto the floor, two or three times per occasion. He administered judo chops to her face and body. When finished, he sent her flying down the stairs again, and when she was down there, he banged her head against the wall.

Johnny also rammed Sylvia against the wall, and he also administered some of the spankings at the request of his mother. But most of the time he used his fists. He kicked her in the leg, and, in the basement, he ground his shoe on Sylvia's bare foot, giving her a blister.

As it became apparent to Gertrude and Paula that

any spread of information about Sylvia might prove embarrassing to them, they formulated instructions to the other children—especially Jenny—not to volunteer any conversation about Sylvia, and to explain to any inquisitive souls that Sylvia had been detained at the Juvenile Center. When Jenny forgot these instructions once and mentioned to church friends that her sister was at home, the younger girls tattled on her and she got the board.

Judy Duke was told "your ass is grass" if she revealed anything.

It was a week or a week and a half before Sylvia's death that Jenny began to worry seriously about her sister. But she believed Gertrude would eventually get Sylvia some medical attention. This was their home, and Mrs. Wright was responsible for them. Jenny had been beaten enough herself to get in the habit of doing what Gertrude said. The thought of going to the police for help never occurred to the crippled, 15-year-old child.

The sickly, doped-up Gertrude still felt well enough in that last week to clobber Sylvia with a board about four times, burn her with cigarettes on the arms, back and legs in about fifteen places, and shove her down the basement stairs several times.

Johnny Baniszewski kept teasing Sylvia and tying and gagging her whenever necessary. Once she was tied in the basement, her hands bound to the stairway railing above her, her feet left barely touching the floor.

All the while, Sylvia slowly was starving. She

took one meal of donuts and water about October 19. A day or two later, she passed out on the living room floor. Stephanie applied a cold, wet rag to Sylvia's forehead, but she was out for nearly 20 minutes. Stephanie and Johnny helped Sylvia to the mattress in the back bedroom upstairs.

Gertrude and Paula decided they ought to have some justification for Sylvia's punishment if some snoopy nurse or other official pestered them again. They instructed Sylvia to write the letter to her parents on school paper, setting out her fifteen confessions of misconduct. Sylvia cooperated. She was too weak and hungry to resist.

It was not as though Sylvia had nothing at all to eat. In the basement, Mrs. Wright had told her son Johnny to "go get some shit." The boy found one of baby Denny's Pampers in a sack in the corner, and it was rubbed into her mouth. Then Sylvia was given a half-cup of water and told to make it last the rest of the day. A day or two later, the water was replaced with a cup of urine.

Sylvia was being punished for eating a sandwich in the park when the others had none. Marie had recalled that a month or two ago, she and Sylvia had met Sylvia's sister Dianna in the park. Sylvia had mentioned that she was hungry, and Dianna had given her a sandwich. This was the first the others had heard about it. Paula, infuriated, clasped her hands about Sylvia's throat and squeezed for half a minute.

"Why didn't you tell me about this?" Gertrude demanded of Sylvia.

"I was afraid you'd give me a whipping," the poor girl responded when she was able to regain her breath.

She was right, but that would not have been half as bad as what she got when Gertrude now found out much later. Gertrude whacked her on the back and back of the head five or six times with the paddle. Sylvia screamed.

She went without supper that night. Jenny did not feel like eating, and she offered hers to Sylvia. Gertrude would not let her have it.

Later, Gertrude and Paula tied Sylvia's hands behind her back and also bound her feet, then dumped her into the bathtub filled with scalding water. Sylvia fainted.

Sylvia got some supper that night, Friday, October 22—some soup in a small bowl. "Start eating," John instructed, "with your fingers." Sylvia tried, but she was not given enough time to finish.

It was decided that Sylvia should have another chance to show her manners in bed. At Gertrude's instructions, Johnny, Coy and Stephanie tied Sylvia to the bed. "You can't go to the bathroom," Gertrude explained with unchallenged logic, "until you've learned not to wet the bed." When the others had gone downstairs, Sylvia whispered to Jenny for a glass of water. She drank it and fell asleep. She wet the bed that night. The next morning, she faced the longest—and last—weekend of her short life.

8

THE LONGEST WEEKEND

SYLVIA'S DAY began with another empty Pepsi bottle. Worse indignities followed.

She got a brief respite when Gertrude and Johnny took off in a Red Cab about 11 a.m. Gertrude had said she was going to the doctor's office. Worried about the possibility of going to the hospital for her bronchitis and her nerves, and blaming it all on the presence of Jenny and Sylvia, she told Jenny before she left: "Jenny, if I have to go to the hospital, you're going to be in as much trouble as Sylvia."

Richard Hobbs stopped over about 1 p.m., shortly after Gertrude had returned home. Gertrude, the asthmatic bronchitis sufferer, was seated at the kitchen table smoking as Hobbs asked her how she felt. She replied she was not feeling well. "I'm having a hard time breathing."

Jenny, Jimmy, Shirley and Marie also were in the room. Jenny and Marie were making plans to rake leaves that afternoon to earn some money. Hobbs was surprised to learn that Sylvia was in the basement;

Gertrude had told him she was at the Juvenile Center. She told him this time that Sylvia had returned home the week before. Ricky had not been in the house for several days.

Gertrude called Sylvia up from the basement. The girl trudged up the stairs. Wearing a tan pair of Bermuda shorts and a light blouse, she appeared listless, and she sported a number of bruises and patchy sores. Gertrude ordered her to stand in the corner, between the doors to the basement and to the dining room.

"Do you know how to put on a tattoo, Ricky?" the woman asked.

"Yes, I guess so," the boy replied.

"Do you know what a tattoo is, Sylvia?" Gertrude asked.

"Yes, ma'am."

"Well," the woman snapped at Sylvia, "you have branded my daughters; now I am going to brand you." And then, to the others: "She's a prostitute, and she's proud of it; so we'll just put it on her stomach."

Mrs. Wright instructed her younger daughters to bring her a sewing needle.

Stephanie, who had been out of school sick a couple of days, was asleep in the front room.

"Take your clothes off, Sylvia," Gertrude ordered. The girl hesitated. Gertrude ripped Sylvia's blouse and shorts off, and the girl stood naked in the corner.

Gertrude pulled up a chair and began to carve

with the sewing needle. She managed to carve a large block "I," an apostrophe, and the first leg of the "M," then turned away. "You take over, Ricky," she said, handing him the needle. "I'm getting sick."

She started for the front bedroom, where Stephanie was sleeping.

"Wait," yelled Ricky. "How do you spell prostitute?"

Gertrude sat down and wrote out the entire message on a piece of paper: "I'M A PROSTITUTE AND PROUD OF IT!" Then she sent Jenny to the grocery.

Before Hobbs resumed the tattoo, he asked Marie to strike a match. He held the needle in the flame to sterilize it.

Then he continued the tattoo, etching in steady, short strokes. Sylvia, past the point of crying, gritted her teeth and moaned. The Hobbs boy struck her with the back of his hand whenever she flinched. The etching brought blood to the surface of the skin.

Hobbs had just about finished when Jenny returned from the store. Soon, there was a knock on the door. The mischievous, cherubic face of Randy Lepper showed through the glass. Ricky, Jenny and Shirley hustled Sylvia to the basement; Gertrude said she did not want Randy to see Sylvia naked. After she was partially clothed again, Gertrude called them upstairs to show Randy the work of art.

Randy asked about the tattoo and the bruises. Gertrude said Sylvia had been to a sex party.

About 15 minutes later, Ricky and Shirley got

around to branding her. They had taken Sylvia back
to the basement. "Look for something we can print
an 'S' with, Shirley," Ricky instructed.

Shirley hunted around through the basement rub-
ble and brought Ricky a three-foot crowbar and a
smaller anchor bolt. Hobbs selected the anchor bolt.
By applying half of the circular hook-end twice, he
reasoned, they could print the "S."

The matches Shirley held were heating her fingers faster than they heated the anchor bolt; so
Ricky set fire to some newspapers in the large sink
and heated the hook end to a glowing red. Sylvia,
who had begged him to quit during the tattooing,
squirmed. Hobbs struck her on the chest with the
back of his hand several times and told her to lie still.
She obeyed, gritting her teeth. Hobbs applied the
first loop. Shirley applied the second.

Either Hobbs applied his half backward, or Shirley misunderstood that she was to apply the lower
loop instead of the upper. In any event, both loops
pointed the same direction, and Sylvia wound up
with a freshly burned-in "3" on her chest, just above
the "prostitute" message. Ricky had at first handed
Jenny the bolt, asking her to do the other loop. She
had handed it back, saying, "No, I ain't going to
burn her." Shirley and Ricky took Sylvia upstairs to
show Gertrude their work.

"Sylvia, what are you going to do now?" the
woman chided. "You can't get married now. What
are you going to do?"

Sylvia did not answer.

"You're proud of it, aren't you, Sylvia?" the woman continued.

It was after 4 p.m. Richard Hobbs, tired from a hard day's work, decided to get on home.

Coy Hubbard was there later and tied Sylvia up in the basement. Then he banged her against the wall six or seven times. Sylvia's day was not over yet.

Mrs. Lepper came over to bring Randy home. A later visitor that night was John Baniszewski Sr., who brought his children a police dog to protect them. Baniszewski did not go inside the house. It was about 9 p.m.

Sylvia was still in the basement, confiding to her sister.

"Jenny, I know you don't want me to die." Her voice was faint; the words came slow. "But I'm going to die. I can tell."

"Well, don't die, Sylvia," her sister pleaded. Jenny felt helpless. But she knew Gertrude would not let Sylvia die—she thought.

Stephanie, still in bed in the front room, spoke briefly to Sylvia about a half-hour later as Sylvia ascended the stairs to the bathroom. There was not much to say. The atmosphere in the house was ominous; a tenseness filled every corner.

The temperature outside was 32 degrees when the sun cracked the darkness Sunday morning. Sylvia had been allowed to sleep upstairs that night; she lay in pain on the mattress on the floor of the bedroom.

In the afternoon, Gertrude and Stephanie bathed Sylvia. It was a warm bath, not a scalding one.

Then Gertrude and Paula dictated to Sylvia the note in which she was to explain that a gang of boys had "got what they wanted" from her and left her in her battered and bruised condition. Sylvia began, "Dear Mom and Dad . . ."

"No," Gertrude intervened inexplicably. "To Mr. and Mrs. Likens."

Gertrude talked of getting rid of Sylvia, of dumping her someplace.

Meanwhile, Johnny had some more fun. He tied Sylvia up in the basement, torture rack fashion, again. As she was suspended, Gertrude offered her some crackers and water. Sylvia turned them down. "Give it to the dog," she said. "I don't want it."

She had lost her will to live. Gertrude would not have it. She smashed her fist into Sylvia's stomach. The crackers were forced into the girl's swollen mouth. Then Johnny got in a few licks. Their fun would not last much longer.

9

DEATH OF TWO WOMEN

IT WAS early Sunday morning—9:30 a.m.—when Mrs. Juanita Hobbs was wheeled into Community Hospital for the last time. Her family at 310 North Denny Street knew she was dying; she had at that time only two weeks to live. She had been beset with cancer about a year, but her family clung desperately to hope.

Woodrow Hobbs grimly faced the task of bringing up their nine children alone. He and Mrs. Hobbs had always tried to give the five boys and four girls correct moral training, and it made no difference that the children felt their parents were strict at times.

None of the children had been in serious trouble.

Fourteen-year-old Ricky, the seventh born, showed particular promise. He was bright and about to make the honor roll at Howe High School. He was especially skilled at drawing and had ideas of becoming an electronics technician. He had attended the Grace Methodist Church Sunday school since childhood and had begun participating in the Methodist Youth Fellowship that year.

Ricky had numerous friends at school, and the adults in the neighborhood liked him too. He was known to have shoveled snow and run errands for neighbors without asking a dime.

When Mrs. Hobbs was taken to the hospital Sunday, October 24, neither she nor her husband was aware that Ricky was acquainted with a large family called the Baniszewskis. She did not know her son had carved the words "I'm a prostitute and proud of it!" on a girl's belly the day before.

When Mrs. Hobbs died November 8, 1965, at the age of 43, a day after her son's 15th birthday, she was not aware that Ricky was under arrest, being held without bond on a charge of murder.

That same Sunday night she had entered the hospital, October 24, 1965, two doors down the street, on a mattress on the grubby floor of an upstairs bedroom, someone else lay dying. But no one had the idea she was going to die, unless her utterance to her sister the night before came from a premonition that she, herself, knew.

She had the words "I'm a prostitute and proud of it!" freshly carved into her belly; above that, a red, ugly "3." The young woman was 16 years old, soon to be 17. Her name was Sylvia. Mrs. Hobbs had slightly more than two weeks to live; Miss Likens had slightly more than two days. Mrs. Hobbs' condition already was terminal; Sylvia's was not, so far as anyone knew. But the rapid series of events that were to occur to her in those next two days, some of them already described as part of her longest weekend, were to bring her to a moribund state much quicker than her 43-year-old neighbor.

Sylvia was somewhat recovered by Monday evening, enough to climb the stairs to the second story, take a bath and chat with Stephanie. It was then, as she saw Sylvia naked in the bathroom, that Stephanie first realized Sylvia had been branded. Stephanie's mother, who said Ricky had done the tattooing and branding, assured her daughter that the words would fade from Sylvia's skin in time.

That was doubtful, but it was an academic proposition anyway. There was no time. And Gertrude, who had been to her doctor that day for treatment for vomiting and a nervous rash covering her face and chest, was in no mood to give Sylvia's wounds time to heal.

Gertrude knew she was in trouble, and she resented Sylvia for it. She slapped the girl; Johnny punched her. Randy Lepper walked into the room and watched them. Gertrude suggested they lose Sylvia and call the police to go looking for her. She picked up a chair to swing at Sylvia, but it broke as she swung clumsily. Gertrude's dope-induced clumsiness also accounted for a black eye she gave herself as she swung the paddle at Sylvia and missed.

The thought of taking Sylvia somewhere and losing her obsessed Mrs. Wright as the group drifted into the front room. She instructed Sylvia's sister Jenny to run upstairs and get dressed. "You and Johnny are going to blindfold her and take her to Jimmy's Forest," she said.

Sylvia, for once, panicked. She made it as far as the front porch, but Gertrude dragged her back inside. Worried about the girl's unhealthy look, Mrs. Wright tried to make her eat two pieces of toast. "I can't swallow," Sylvia mumbled through her swollen mouth. As though she could force Sylvia to eat, Gertrude whipped her across the face with a brass curtain rod, again and again until the pieces were bent into right angles.

Coy Hubbard finished work at Laughner's Cafeteria at 8:30 p.m., and he stopped in at Mrs. Wright's on his way home to get his exercise. His appearance stopped the sport for a while because his one hard blow with a broomstick knocked Sylvia unconscious. Mrs. Wright dragged the motionless girl to the basement. It was the last time Coy Hubbard saw Sylvia alive.

A half-hour past midnight, a car with two occupants pulled to the curb of the half-lit, somewhat quieted New York Street. When the motor died, the woman and her husband heard a scraping sound coming from the direction of the Baniszewski house. A strange time to shovel coal.

Mr. and Mrs. Vermillion went on inside their own house next door. But the noise from the neighbors' house was not getting any softer, and an occasional shout rose above the scraping. Mrs. Vermillion's combination of annoyance and curiosity guided her outdoors; she saw a light in the Baniszewski basement, and she decided that the basement was the source of the noise.

Inside, the younger children, including Jenny, had gone to bed.

The noise continued. "Well, I just may have to call the police to stop that," the neighbor woman mused. But it stopped—at 3 a.m. What happened in the basement that night was known only to Gertrude and to Sylvia; one of them never told, and the other never had a chance to.

Jenny did not see her sister before school the next morning, but she came home for lunch shortly before noon and, after fixing two pieces of toast, descended the basement steps. Sylvia was half-sitting, half-lying on the floor. She refused the toast. Jenny could not make out the words Sylvia was trying to say.

Before Jenny returned home from the afternoon school session, Mrs. Wright had Sylvia propped up in the kitchen, trying to feed her some milk and do-nuts. She had thrown Sylvia to the floor in frustra-tion, but had propped her back up in the chair and had handed her the donuts and glass of milk. Sylvia mumbled something unintelligible and threw the glass of milk to the floor, spastically. Shirley, who had been home all day with a cold, watched, not knowing what to say.

Gertrude gave Sylvia another glass of milk. Syl-via attempted to raise it to her mouth but again lost control of her arm. She was taken back down to the basement.

She was lying on the floor of the basement when

Paula came home from her new job at a downtown cafeteria. Sylvia just lay there, moaning, mumbling. She tried to recite her ABC's, but could not get past D: "A, B, C, . . . D, . . . ," and over again. Gertrude was shouting at her to clean herself up. She had moved her bowels.

"If you don't get up," Paula said, "I'll give you a broad jump."

Other children gathered in the basement; Jenny had arrived home shortly after 3:30. Ricky Hobbs stopped in to say hello; he was still in his school clothes. Sylvia managed to look around and point at Hobbs and Mrs. Wright. "You're Ricky," she drawled, "and you're Gertie. . . ."

"Shut up," Gertrude snapped. "You know who I am."

"All my teeth feel loose," Sylvia said. She had a rotten pear in her hand but was having trouble biting into it.

"Don't you remember, Sylvia?" Jenny asked. "Your front tooth was knocked out when you were seven."

Sylvia collapsed on the floor near the steps. Infuriated, Gertrude stepped onto the girl's face, first one foot, then the other, and just stood there a moment.

Jenny had hoped to earn some money that afternoon, and shortly she left the house with a rake. She was never to see her sister and companion alive again.

Marie had stopped down in the basement. "Hi, Sylvia," she said quietly, waving her hand slightly.

Sylvia's hand moved slightly, and she tried to say

something, but it appeared to be too much effort. Marie left with Jenny.

"You faker!" Gertrude shouted at Sylvia. "Clean yourself up."

At Gertrude's request, Randy Lepper had brought over his parents' garden hose so that Gertrude could clean out the basement, as he understood it. When he reached the bottom of the steps, he saw Johnny turning the hose on Sylvia, laughing. Someone had covered the girl's body with Trend detergent to aid in the cleansing.

Gertrude, who had climbed the basement steps back to the kitchen, saw that Stephanie was home now and explained that Sylvia had had an accident in her shorts. She asked Stephanie to wash Sylvia. It was about 5 p.m.

Stephanie dropped her books, trotted down the stairs, and saw her brother already washing Sylvia, with the hose. Sylvia, half-lying, half-sitting, was mumbling something incoherent. "Turn off that hose!" Stephanie instructed her brother. She intended to carry Sylvia upstairs for a bath but found her too heavy. Stephanie, worried, began to cry.

Ricky Hobbs had done his homework, changed clothes and eaten dinner, and he was on his way back to the Baniszewski house. He was a little curious about Sylvia.

When he opened the Baniszewskis' back door and walked in about 5:30, he slipped down the basement stairs. Gertrude was slumped against the wall, crying; Stephanie, cuddling Sylvia, was crying too.

"What's the matter?" the boy asked. Stephanie said she thought Sylvia might be dead.

But Hobbs detected short, labored breaths from Sylvia and, with Stephanie's help, managed to drag the girl up to the kitchen. Her skin was cold, and someone wrapped her in a blanket. Hobbs thought she was having extreme trouble breathing and began to apply pressure respiration.

Stephanie ran upstairs to turn on the water for a warm bath. Soon Johnny, who had finished hosing off the basement floor, called from upstairs that the bath was ready. Stephanie grabbed Sylvia's feet, and Hobbs grabbed her under the arms. They started up the stairs. Near the top, Sylvia's wet, slippery body fell from Hobbs' grasp, and her head banged on the steps.

Gertrude followed them upstairs. "She's faking!" she repeated. "She'll be all right!"

But when Stephanie began to undress Sylvia for the bath, Gertrude ordered them to dump Sylvia in the tub with her clothes on. "Hurry!" she said. Sylvia managed to groan. "I wish my daddy was here," she moaned faintly.

After the bath, Ricky and Stephanie dried Sylvia and dressed her in warmer clothes, a sweater and pedal-pushers. They laid her on the mattress in the bedroom.

Gertrude followed them into the bedroom, shouting frantically, "Faker! Faker!" She picked up a book and slapped Sylvia hard on the side of the head.

Hobbs practically pushed the hysterical Mrs. Wright down the stairs.

Shirley brought up some hot tea and asked how Sylvia was doing. "Oh, she'll be all right," Stephanie assured, but she had already suggested to Ricky to call a doctor.

Stephanie raised Sylvia's head and brushed the girl's hair back; she seemed to revive somewhat. "Oh, take me home, Stephanie," she pleaded.

Suddenly, she stopped breathing. Hobbs came back in and put his ear to her chest, listening for a heartbeat. "Do you know how to give mouth-to-mouth respiration?" he asked Stephanie.

"Yes," she said.

"Okay, give it to her," Hobbs said.

Gertrude wandered back into the room, screaming. "Stop screaming and get out!" Stephanie ordered. She began the mouth-to-mouth resuscitation; and Sylvia began breathing once more.

Stephanie understood that Ricky had gone to call the police instead of a doctor, and she was hoping they would get there soon with a mechanical resuscitator. She still was expecting police to revive Sylvia when they rushed into the room. But to her dismay, they did nothing. Sylvia was dead.

10

INDICTED FOR MURDER

IF THE general citizenry of Indianapolis was shocked by the horror of the murder, detectives and attorneys were at least equally shocked at the casualness and lack of remorse shown by the children who participated in it. Child after child, when asked to explain why he or she participated, said simply, "Gertie told me to."

Did Gertie Wright have a hypnotic evil eye? Hardly. More than hypnotic, she was a hypochondriac, a whiny medicine hound. But she was the authority in her own household, and she had a way of getting what she wanted done. Children harboring some pent-up hostility, egged on by slanders on Sylvia Likens, encouraged by the mob psychology of seeing others mistreat her, found that their own mistreatment of Sylvia was sanctioned—even prescribed—by the only adult in the house.

But their behavior was not sanctioned by society in general, or by the law in particular. And when the police closed in on them, the children found they no longer had even Mrs. Wright to back them up. For the haggard woman appealed to her physical ailments as evidence she could not possibly have been able to cause Sylvia any great harm. She told police she was in bed sick most of October and did not even see Sylvia much of that time. If anyone harmed Sylvia, she concluded, it must have been the children.

The first one questioned in the case, after Jenny Likens, was Richard Hobbs. Ricky, when questioned at the scene, had gone along with Gertrude's little tale—that Sylvia had come to the back door that evening, battered and bruised.

Asked what he was doing there, the boy told police, "I'm a friend of Gertrude's." He mentioned also that his father did not allow him to stay out late at night, so police let him go home for the time being. He watched television a while before going to bed shortly before 9 p.m., the time at which police rapped on the door and told construction worker Woodrow Hobbs that his 14-year-old son would have to come along with them.

At police headquarters, on the fourth floor of a six-story wing off the towering City-County Building, the boy talked freely and more truthfully after Detective Sgt. Kaiser told him Jenny had implicated him. Ricky's father had always instructed him to be truthful.

The next day, when the defendants appeared for arraignment in Municipal Court, Kaiser advised the elder Hobbs he had better get an attorney for the boy. "Sgt. Kaiser," the man replied, "if my boy's involved in this thing, I want him to tell you the truth and cooperate." Kaiser took a signed confession from the boy that afternoon, in which Ricky admitted his participation in the tattooing and branding, adding that he hit Sylvia 10 or 15 times on the chest with the back of his hand.

"Why didn't Sylvia get up and leave?" a newspaper reporter asked the Hobbs boy later. "Was she a masochist?"

"To tell you the truth," the boy replied, "I didn't know Sylvia that well. It was just a casual relationship."

He had just happened to be there when Mrs. Wright told him to tattoo Sylvia, and he did it. It was that simple.

Next to talk to Kaiser was Mrs. Wright. Kaiser learned that her true legal name was Baniszewski, and she was to be known as Gertrude Baniszewski throughout the court proceedings.

She fidgeted, and she told the detective she was being treated by a doctor for nerves and asthma. She denied all knowledge of Sylvia's mistreatment. Kaiser slapped a preliminary murder charge on her, told her she could get an attorney if she wished, and said he would see her in court the next day.

Meanwhile, all six Baniszewski children were taken to the Juvenile Center and held as material witnesses.

Hobbs was transferred from the county jail to the detention ward of Marion County General Hospital when police learned he was a diabetic. He would reside there, chained to an iron bed, until the end of his trial seven months later.

He was permitted to visit his mother in Community Hospital before she died, and precautions were taken to ensure that she did not become aware he was in custody. He was permitted also to attend her funeral November 11, and precautions were taken then to ensure he made no attempt to escape.

Kaiser talked to Mrs. Baniszewski again Wednesday, October 27, after she and Hobbs appeared in Municipal Court Room 6. Their case was continued until the following Monday, November 1.

The woman had not brought her attorney. She sat down at 9:50 a.m. in a small, bare room with Kaiser and Lt. Spurgeon D. Davenport, a skilled and debonair black man who, at that time, was chief of homicide investigations.

She admitted then, "I know the kids have been mistreating Sylvia." Then she admitted that she had made Sylvia sleep in the basement—"only three times"—because she had wet the bed.

"Isn't the reason she wet the bed," Kaiser suggested, "because you injured her kidneys when you hit her on the back with that paddle?"

But she knew nothing like that, she insisted. She did recall once telling Johnny, "Go get some shit and make her eat it." She also recalled burning Sylvia on the arm with a cigarette, once, about a month ago.

But it was the children who mistreated Sylvia, she said. "Paula did most of the damage; she broke her wrist once hitting Sylvia. And I saw Coy Hubbard beat her up once. Coy Hubbard did a lot of the beating."

But Mrs. Baniszewski (Kaiser learned that was her legal name when he talked to her again Friday, October 29) insisted she had done nothing wrong and therefore did not need an attorney. She also saw no reason to sign a statement for police, and she did not.

Who was Coy Hubbard? Police heard that name and a few others mentioned as they talked to the principals in the crime. They soon found out who Hubbard was, and officers from the juvenile detail were sent to Howe High School early that afternoon. He was whisked out of class at 3 p.m., into a squad car and downtown to police headquarters, where he was questioned by Sgt. Don R. Campbell and Lt. William Crossen of juvenile branch.

Like Hobbs, Hubbard declined calling for his parents. Police notified his mother at work by telephone, and she hastened to her boy's side; but she did not get to him in time to keep him from talking. In his signed statement, Hubbard admitted: "I hit her with my hand. . . . I do not remember why . . . but Mrs. Wright had spanked her. . . . I flipped Sylvia on the floor; I think I did this because of something she said about Stephanie. . . . I burned Sylvia on the arm with a match. . . . Last week I was at the house and I took Sylvia down two or three steps of the basement stairs and put her hands behind her and pushed her the rest of the way down."

Earlier that day, two other juvenile officers—Sgt. Leo Gentry and Policewoman Harriet Sanders—had talked to Paula and Johnny Baniszewski. Like Hubbard, they were held only on the juvenile delinquency charge of "injury to person" at that time.

Paula, in her signed statement, admitted, "In three months, I beat Sylvia Likens with the police belt about 25 times on the butt." She admitted breaking her wrist on Sylvia's jaw, giving Sylvia a black eye, and pushing her down the stairs two or three times. "Johnny teased Sylvia and made fun of her," Paula added. Paula emphatically denied being pregnant.

Johnny, in his signed statement, admitted, "Once my mother let me take her upstairs and spank her, but most of the time I used my fists. . . . I used matches and Mom used cigarettes to burn her."

Did he gag her? "Yes, Mom told me to so that Sylvia wouldn't make too much noise when we hit her. . . . Some of the time I did this [hit Sylvia] for something she had done."

Johnny listed something else police wanted—names. Others who had beaten Sylvia, he said, included Paula Baniszewski, Stephanie Baniszewski, Marie Baniszewski, Shirley Baniszewski, Anna Siscoe, Judy Duke, Darlene McGuire, Randy Lepper, Mike Monroe, Coy Hubbard and Richard Hobbs.

The next day, Thursday, October 28, police arrested Anna Siscoe and Mike Monroe. On Friday, October 29, they arrested Judy Duke and Randy Lepper. All were charged with "injury to person."

On the top floor of the six-story police wing of the City-County Building in Indianapolis were the city's four traffic and misdemeanor courts, Municipal

Court Rooms 3, 4, 5 and 6. Through their doors passed the cream of society and the scum of the earth, from executives appearing on speeding charges to notorious felons on their way to grand jury investigations or higher courts.

Each courtroom in the modern, new building had a large gallery with seats for more than a hundred spectators and standing room for nearly that many more. Usually the seats were occupied by persons waiting to be arraigned or tried on minor offenses; seldom were all the seats in use.

But at 2 p.m. Monday, November 1, 1965, defendants had to stand in line outside Municipal Court Room 6, as curious spectators had filled the gallery long before that. The city's curious, many of them from the several thousand workers in the City-County Building, had come to get a glimpse of the sadistic Likens murderers.

An attorney in the crowd remarked, "If some of these people had been this concerned about Sylvia earlier, she probably would be alive today."

Dianna Shoemaker, Sylvia's older sister, also was in the crowd. She told a newspaper reporter she had gone to Mrs. Baniszewski's house about a month before to see Sylvia, but the woman had refused to let her in, saying, "I've got permission not to let you see her."

She said she saw Jenny on the street about two weeks later and stopped to talk, but Jenny said, "I can't talk to you or I'll get in trouble."

After a brief hearing, Judge Harry F. Zaklan ordered that Mrs. Baniszewski, Paula, Stephanie and Johnny Baniszewski and Richard Hobbs be held without bond on murder charges for grand jury investigation. Coy Hubbard's case was continued until November 24. Anna Siscoe, Judy Duke, Randy Lepper and Mike Monroe were to be kept in the Juvenile Center on delinquency charges.

Hobbs was kept in the hospital detention ward. The others were sent to the Marion County Jail.

Mr. and Mrs. Lester Likens were sleeping comfortably in their hotel room in Jacksonville, Florida, the night of October 26, 1965. They had been doing well with their lunch stand in the Florida carnival, and in a week they would be back home in Indiana. It was the last fair of the season. They had saved enough money on the northern tour to buy their own stand by the time they headed for Florida.

The telephone rudely interrupted their slumber. The caller was D. L. Burton, a former neighbor in Indianapolis. The news was bad. Likens could not believe it.

In semi-shock, he and his wife, Betty, climbed into their clothes and caught a taxi back to the fairgrounds, from where a friend gave them a lift to the airport. They arrived in Indianapolis to claim their daughter's mangled body about midday on Wednesday, October 27.

In police headquarters, Likens asked to see the signed statement of his other daughter, Jenny. He began reading it but could not finish. Tears welled in his eyes, then poured forth.

Late-afternoon shadows shaded the Russell & Hitch Funeral Home in Lebanon, Indiana. The lilt of children's laughter could be heard faintly outside, from the direction of the school. Inside, children and adults wept. It was Friday, October 29. The Rev. Louis Gibson was assuring his listeners that the soul of Sylvia Likens was in heaven.

"We all have our time," the preacher reminded, "but we won't suffer like our little sister suffered during the last days of her life." He strode toward the gray open casket, whispering, "She has gone to eternity." A portrait of Sylvia taken before her stay at 3850 East New York Street adorned the casket.

A fourteen-car procession followed the hearse to Oak Hill Cemetery on the outskirts of East Lebanon. Mr. and Mrs. Lester Likens and their surviving children rode with Likens' brother Leroy, member of the Rev. Mr. Gibson's congregation at Charity Tabernacle in Indianapolis.

A few more words, a hymn, a tree swaying in the breeze, a few falling leaves—and it was over.

The Likens family returned to the home of Lester's mother, Mrs. Ernest Martin.

Had Sylvia been tortured to death in Lebanon, rather than in Indianapolis, an immediate session of the Boone County grand jury would have been called to investigate the case. But in Marion County, where Indianapolis is the county seat, each case must wait its turn before a hard-working, nearly full-time grand jury.

The six members of the grand jury in the latter half of 1965 were particularly busy. By the time they got around to the Likens case on December 4, they had questioned more than a hundred witnesses in an investigation of the county jail set off by the state's largest daily newspaper, the *Indianapolis Star.*

The *Star*'s first story of its series on the jail appeared October 27, the same day Sylvia's murder was reported, and stole the headlines from the murder—which, under almost any other circumstances, would have been the main story. Later, the jail probe fizzled when the sworn statement of a prisoner was discredited.

The grand jurors also had spent several weeks on an investigation of the state's securities market and the secretary of state's office. The securities business had been muddied by a $2 million stock fraud and by a federal court injunction against a complicated stock promotion, and the youthful secretary of state had admitted receiving campaign contributions—before and after the campaign—from securities dealers whose activities he was supposed to be regulating.

The grand jurors had been concerned also with a bribery case involving a veteran sheriff's detective who had been caught by the county sheriff stuffing a roll of paper money into his pocket that had just been handed to him by an ex-convict.

Another matter on the grand jurors' minds was a child-stealing case against a Tennessee couple who had tentatively adopted an Indianapolis woman's baby, then fled the state with the child when the mother refused to sign the adoption papers.

It seemed that murder was too mundane for the Marion County grand jury. And yet, the grand jury already had returned more than a hundred indictments in routine crime investigations that fall, many of them for murder.

There was a question of whether the Likens case would ever be heard by the present grand jury. The week before the Likens case did reach them, jury members had attempted to resign in a huff after a judge charged them with "whitewashing" the charges levied against the jail by the *Indianapolis Star*. But the two Criminal Court judges refused to let the jurors resign before the end of the court term, December 31.

The day the grand jury's investigation of the Likens case began, the Baniszewski family attorney filed a motion for writ of habeas corpus to get Stephanie Baniszewski released on bond.

The attorney, John R. Hammond, in his motion filed on December 3 in Criminal Court, Division 2, contended that the state had no evidence to support a murder charge against Stephanie. Hammond also contended that it was illegal to hold 15-year-old Stephanie in the county jail because that deprived her of her schooling required by the state's compulsory education law for children under 16.

"How well do you like school?" Judge Saul I. Rabb asked the girl at her hearing four days later.

"Judge," she said, "if school were a man, I'd marry it."

She later was transferred to the county Juvenile Center, where she could attend school.

Stephanie showed her confidence of her innocence by waiving immunity from prosecution and testifying before the grand jury. The investigative body, whose hearings are kept secret by state law, also heard from another 15-year-old girl that day, Jenny Fay Likens. Three policemen testified to round out the December 4 grand jury hearing.

Later, Gertrude Baniszewski also asked to be heard by the grand jury. Her testimony was to embarrass her later. Although grand jury testimony normally is secret, there is a provision for its release. It can be read from at trial to show conflicts between a witness's grand jury testimony and his or her trial testimony.

Grand jury testimony thus can be useful to the state not only for its investigative value, but also for its value in impeaching witnesses and in prosecuting perjury cases. Gertrude Baniszewski found this out the hard way.

There was one slight matter to be disposed of before the grand jury could report on the Likens case. On December 21, Coy Hubbard was bound from Municipal Court Room 6 to the grand jury on a charge of murder.

The grand jury's final report of the year, on December 30, contained two indictments for first-degree murder, one for second-degree murder, one for voluntary manslaughter, one for bribery, one for involuntary manslaughter, three for assault and battery with intent to gratify sexual desires, four for assault and battery with intent to kill, seven for rape, one for sodomy, one for aiding an escape, two for aggravated assault and battery, four for larceny, one for forgery, and one for attempted arson.

Conviction of first-degree murder in Indiana carried a sentence of death in the electric chair or life in prison, as determined by the judge and jury. No woman or child had ever been sentenced to death in Indiana.

One of the first-degree murder indictments returned by the Marion County grand jury on December 30, 1965, named Gertrude Baniszewski, 37 years old; Paula Baniszewski, 17; Stephanie Baniszewski, 15; Johnny Baniszewski, 12; Coy Hubbard, 15, and Richard Hobbs, also then 15—all charged with striking, beating, kicking and otherwise inflicting fatal injuries on one Sylvia Likens—with premeditated malice.

No charges were levied against Anna Siscoe, Judy Duke, Randy Lepper or Mike Monroe. They were released to their parents. Marie, Shirley and Jimmy Baniszewski were placed in separate foster homes by the Marion County Department of Public Welfare.

11

A JUDGE AND FIVE LAWYERS

SALTY OLD Saul Rabb, judge of Criminal Court, Division 2, had been on the bench since the court was created in 1947, except for one four-year term he lost out on in the Democratic landslide of 1958. Lawyers both respected him for his knowledge of the law and despised him for his sarcasm, his particular brand being known in courthouse circles as "the needle."

Rabb was loved by newspaper reporters for his witticisms and his eagerness to help them with a story, and feared by his staff, a bevy of pretty, young girls, one of whom once asked him for permission to go to the restroom.

A tiny, balding man wearing rimless spectacles, Rabb had a reputation for being stern but fair. Characterized as "Judge Saul Stab" at a lawyers' gridiron dinner, Rabb dealt harshly with second offenders and other criminals who showed no promise. But he once reduced an 18-year-old thief's sentence when the lad kissed his mother good-bye in the courtroom. "That shows he's a good boy," the judge quipped.

It was into Rabb's court that the Likens murder indictment was returned. The quotation that hung on the wall of the courtroom—"Justice delayed is justice denied"—was taken seriously in Rabb's court. The only way to stall a trial over a period of years in there was to take a change of judge, and hundreds of new cases were filed in the court every year.

Rabb sensed the special need of a quick trial in the Likens case. In any case, a common defense tactic is to request continuance after continuance; not only does this discourage witnesses from coming to court, but it also tends to fog their memories as the events of the crime are pushed further and further into the past.

Rabb's steadfast denial of bond for the six defendants (within the judge's discretion in a murder case) discouraged their thoughts of delaying the case, and his speedy but studied rulings on a flood of dilatory motions insured that the trial would proceed nearly on schedule.

Cynics said the judge wanted to try the case early to gain maximum publicity from it in time for the primary election in May.

But responsible lawyers observed that no judge would look forward to a case like this one. There would be at least five lawyers to control, and the case would probably run at least that many weeks. It would be tiring, and it would be difficult keeping the jurors admonished as to what they could and could not consider as evidence, with six defendants on trial.

Much of the testimony would be admissible against one defendant, but not against others. Moreover, among the lawyers would be two of the state's most flamboyant advocates, William C. Erbecker and Forrest B. Bowman Jr.

Sensing the conflicts of interest that would arise among the six defendants, Baniszewski family lawyer John R. Hammond had begun to deal his clients out to other lawyers in December. Hammond, young and handsome, had an office in the suburbs and a varied practice in the city. He was sort of a country lawyer in a big town. He had never handled a murder case before, but he knew how to handle this one. The one client he kept for himself was 15-year-old Stephanie, the most likely to be found innocent.

Gertrude's case was given to Erbecker, a shotgun tactician who had been accused of operating just a shade above the law himself; he once had been indicted on a charge of subornation of perjury, a charge that was later dismissed for lack of evidence.

Paula's case was given to George P. Rice Jr., a dignified divorced man. Author of several books, Rice held a Ph.D. in psychology and was a full-time professor of speech at Indianapolis' Butler University before entering law school at the age of 38.

Johnny's case and, later, the case of Coy Hubbard were assumed by Bowman, youthful, squat and impish-looking behind his thick-rimmed spectacles.

Bowman was the junior partner and protégé of attorney Ferdinand Samper, who was running against Rabb for the Republican nomination for Rabb's judgeship.

Bowman showed signs of the thoroughness, the courtroom flair and the occasional oddball tactics that had made Samper, a veteran of fifty murder trials, one of the most conspicuous defense lawyers in the state.

The fifth defense lawyer in the case was James G. Nedeff, for Richard Hobbs. He took Hobbs' case as one of three salaried public defenders in Rabb's court; and as such, he was the only defense lawyer getting paid for his work in the case. None of the defendants had any funds with which to pay an attorney, and the other lawyers had volunteered their services.

These five lawyers kept Judge Rabb busy for several months by filing voluminous preliminary pleadings. Erbecker managed to delay Gertrude's arraignment on the indictment for nearly two months.

The first pleading filed in the case after the indictment was returned was a motion by Erbecker for Mrs. Baniszewski's release on a writ of habeas corpus. In the lengthy pleading, Erbecker contended that his client's "constitutional rights were violated in that she was induced to testify before the grand jury, and the evidence related by her was used to obtain the indictment. . . ."

The pleading had little apparent merit, but it satisfied Erbecker's motives in two ways: (1) It caused a hearing in which the state was forced to produce some of its evidence before the trial, and (2) it was one step in establishing a possible trial court error on which he could base an appeal later.

It was nothing for Erbecker to turn out a fifty-page pleading overnight, complete with constitutional arguments and Supreme Court citations.

One of his specialties was taking Supreme Court appeals for hated convicted felons; at that very time he was keeping a convicted killer of a Marion County deputy sheriff from burning in the electric chair by filing motions for new trial, petitions for permission to file motions for new trial, belated motions for new trial, motions for writ of certiorari by the United States Supreme Court, etc., etc., etc. In many cases involving a confession, he would charge that the defendant's civil rights were violated by police.

Heavyset, nearly bald, and mustached, Erbecker at the time was a candidate for the Democratic nomination for prosecutor. It was his role, he explained, to do anything within the law to help his client.

Soon after Erbecker's habeas corpus petition came the first of a number of bizarre pleadings from Forrest Bowman, attorney for Johnny Baniszewski and Coy Hubbard. It was a motion to quash the indictment against Johnny, who, at 12 years of age, could not be presumed capable of harboring any criminal intent, Bowman argued. The law in Indiana presumed children under 15 to be incapable of criminal intent. What Bowman did not mention, however, was that the law also stated that the presumption of lack of intent can be rebutted by evidence. Only children under seven years of age were protected entirely from prosecution.

Bowman cited also some poor grammar in the indictment in his motion to quash. The indictment charged the defendants with killing Sylvia Likens "by . . . strike, beat and kick" her, instead of "by . . . striking, beating and kicking" her. "It is obvious," Bowman argued in his motion, "that the above allegations, insofar as English grammar is commonly understood, say nothing." But Judge Rabb ruled that the poor grammar was a technical fault only and that the meaning was clear.

As for the charge against Johnny, Bowman argued, "It is an outrageous violation of fundamental fairness and due process of law to prosecute a 12-year-old infant for a felony punishable by death or life imprisonment. . . . The brooding spirit of the common law as well as our constitutional principles of fairness will permit no such legal outrage in the latter half of the 20th Century."

But whether outrageous or not, Judge Rabb ruled that the law does allow such prosecution. Attorneys for the state argued that the crime committed by the 12-year-old infant was far more outrageous than the fact that he was being prosecuted.

January 12, 1966, the date set for arraignments and habeas corpus hearing, soon came. For newsmen and other spectators, it was a preview of the courtroom drama to come.

Under the rule of law applying to habeas corpus proceedings, the state had no right to hold defendants in jail without sufficient evidence to produce a strong presumption of guilt. William Erbecker knew that the state had sufficient evidence against his client, Gertrude Baniszewski, but he wanted to find out what some of it was.

In the courtroom vernacular, Erbecker was "on a fishing expedition." The state's usual tactic in such cases is to present as little evidence as possible but still enough for presumption of guilt. The procedure, however, is for defense lawyers to call in state's witnesses—the ones they know of or can force the prosecution to name—and conduct the questioning. One way the state tries to limit evidence is to produce only a partial list of witnesses.

For whatever reasons, the only eyewitnesses called were Randy Lepper and Judy Duke. Neither possessed a wealth of information, but both produced enough testimony to keep the defendants in jail. Other witnesses at the hearing were the public health nurse, Barbara Sanders; the deputy coroner, Dr. Kebel; the pathologist, Dr. Ellis, and Sgt. Kaiser, armed with signed confessions.

Stephanie Baniszewski also was involved in the habeas corpus hearing, and it was not just a "fishing expedition" for her attorney, John Hammond. He was convinced that the state lacked evidence against Stephanie, and he was there to prove it.

The nurse was first to the witness stand; she described Mrs. Baniszewski's attitude as "resentful and defiant" at the time of her October 15 visit to the house. But the children she saw looked healthy, Mrs. Sanders said.

Next to the stand was Randy Lepper, one of the most interesting witnesses in the case, from the standpoint of courtroom behavior. His impish eyes rolled toward the ceiling as incriminating questions were tossed his way, and he smiled mischievously as he admitted his participation in the crime. Randy testified to seeing Gertrude beat Sylvia; and he said he once saw Sylvia cry, "but no tears came out of her eyes."

"I only seen Stephanie slap her once, real hard," he said, "for undressing before me and Johnny." He may have been referring to the incident of the Pepsi bottle. He said Stephanie made straight A's in school and cried when she was sick and had to stay home.

Equally interesting was Judy Duke. Tall and pretty at 12 years of age, with long, blond hair, she gave strangely tardy responses and sometimes no response at all to attorneys' questions.

"Now, on how many different occasions," Erbecker asked her, "did you see Mrs. Baniszewski strike Sylvia Likens?"

The girl said nothing.

"Occasions," Judge Rabb explained to the young witness, "means times. How many *times* did the woman *hit* her?

"These are children, Mr. Erbecker," the judge said. "Talk to them in language they understand."

Judy knew what "times" meant. "Oh, about 12 times," she said.

"Now, isn't it a fact," Erbecker questioned, "you never saw Mrs. Baniszewski, at any time, do anything that would injure the victim in any material way?"

Again, no response.

And again, a suggestion from the judge. " 'Isn't it a fact,' " he said, "is *lawyers'* talk. Talk to them in *children's* talk.

"Did you ever see Mrs. Baniszewski *hurt* Sylvia?" the judge rephrased the question for Judy.

John Hammond elicited testimony to show Stephanie's lack of participation. "They sent her to the store or something," Judy told him. "She never knew anything about it."

"A real nice girl," Hammond suggested.

Dr. Kebel testified that Sylvia may have been in too advanced shock to offer much resistance or many tears in her final hours. He testified that the blow on the head was probably "the major contributing cause" of Sylvia's death but that it might just have been "the straw that broke the camel's back."

He noted that Sylvia was "well developed sexually."

Dr. Ellis testified that Sylvia's fingernails' being broken backward indicated a desperate scratching motion.

Sgt. Kaiser read statements implicating all defendants.

Erbecker described Mrs. Baniszewski as a nervous wreck and said she should be free on bond to be able to help him gather evidence.

But Rabb denied both Mrs. Baniszewski's and Stephanie's petitions. He said the evidence reminded him of the D. C. Stephenson case. Stephenson, head of the Ku Klux Klan in its heyday in Indiana in the 1920's, was convicted of murdering a young Indianapolis woman even though he administered no fatal injury to her. There was evidence that he kidnapped her and forced her to submit to sadism and sexual perversion. In despair at not being able to escape, the young woman took poison and died from it. Stephenson was convicted on the theory that his actions induced her to poison herself and the theory that he neglected to seek medical aid for her although he knew her condition.

Stephanie, heartbroken, was joined by her father as she left the courtroom. "But, Daddy," she sobbed, "I just can't stand to have people think I'd do something like this."

"Nobody ever accused her of doing anything to this girl," her attorney had said during the grand jury investigation. "She's an exceptional girl."

The next day, January 13, 1966, Judge Rabb did order the transfer of Stephanie and Johnny to the Juvenile Center. The same day, Richard Hobbs and Stephanie became the first to be arraigned in the case. Both pleaded not guilty. Arraignments of the others were postponed.

The tattooed abdomen of Sylvia Likens.

Courtesy Indianapolis Police Department

Forrest B. Bowman Jr., attorney for Johnny Baniszewski and Coy Hubbard.

Courtesy The Indianapolis Star

The basement where Sylvia Likens spent her last days.

Courtesy The Indianapolis News, photo by Nick Longworth

Dianna Shoemaker, Jenny and Sylvia Likens' older sister.

Courtesy The Indianapolis News

Gertrude Baniszewski.

Courtesy The Indianapolis Star

William C. Erbecker, attorney for Gertrude Baniszewski.

Courtesy The Indianapolis Star

Richard Hobbs and Gertrude Baniszewski in court.

Courtesy Detective Cases magazine

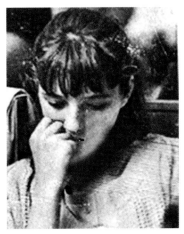

Jenny Likens.

Courtesy The Indianapolis Star

Coy Hubbard.

*Courtesy
The Indianapolis News*

The house at 3850 East New York Street, and the Hobbs' house, on Denny Street, at far right.

Courtesy The Indianapolis News

Johnny Baniszewski and mother, Gertrude, at sentencing.

Courtesy The Indianapolis Star; photo by William A. Oates

Marie Baniszewski.

*Courtesy
The Indianapolis Star*

Detective Sgt.
William E. Kaiser.

Courtesy Paul Kaiser

Deathbed: the upstairs mattress on which Sylvia Likens died.

Courtesy Associated Press

Leroy K. New,
Chief Trial Deputy
Prosecutor for
Marion County,
Indiana.

Courtesy Leroy New

James G. Nedeff,
attorney for Richard
Hobbs.

*Courtesy The
Indianapolis Star*

Sylvia Likens.

Paula Baniszewski.

Courtesy
The Indianapolis Star

Judge Saul I. Rabb.

Courtesy
The Indianapolis Star

Sylvia Likens.

Marjorie Wessner, Deputy Prosecutor, Marion County, Indiana.

Courtesy The Indianapolis Star

The author in 1966.

George P. Rice Jr.

Courtesy The Indianapolis Star

A more recent photo of the author.

Mrs. Baniszewski had assumed a brief bit of glamor during the hearing. She came to court wearing a luxuriant bouffant hairdo. But her hair was back to its straggly self at her next appearance.

A reporter, Rick Johnson, of the *Indianapolis Star*, had learned that the woman was getting hairdos in return for knitting she did for jail matrons. This violated jail rules against "trafficking with inmates," and Johnson's little item in the *Star* put an end to it.

The next avenue of defense for the attorneys was the insanity route.

George Rice was the first to file a "suggestion of insanity," which he did for his client, Paula Baniszewski, on January 11, 1966. It stated "that petitioner [Rice] is a doctor of philosophy, said degree awarded him by Cornell University in psychology. That after several hours of conference with the defendant herein, petitioner believes and has reason to believe that the defendant does not understand the nature of the offense with which she is charged and does not have the ability to assist actively in the preparation of her defense."

There are two considerations of criminal sanity in the law. The first is a matter of "competence," or present comprehension. If a defendant is judged by the court not to comprehend the nature of the charge or mentally unable to assist his or her attorney, he or she can be declared incompetent and committed to a state mental hospital until judged competent again. Such a commitment could delay a trial indefinitely, even until all witnesses have died. Once the defendant is judged competent again, he or she must stand trial.

The second consideration is sanity at the time of the crime—that is, if the defendant did not understand the nature of his or her actions at the time of the crime, did not know right from wrong, or did not have sufficient will power to control his or her actions, he or she is not legally responsible, and must be acquitted.

In both sanity considerations, the judge must appoint physicians to examine the defendant; the physicians then may give testimony in court. It is up to the judge to decide whether a defendant is competent to stand trial; it is up to the jury during the trial whether a defendant was sane or legally responsible for his actions.

The suggestion of insanity or noncomprehension is one of a defense attorney's means of forcing the issue and getting the court to appoint examining physicians, usually psychiatrists.

Erbecker followed Rice two days later with a "suggestion of insanity" for Mrs. Baniszewski.

Judge Rabb ordered Mrs. Baniszewski to be taken to Marion County General Hospital January 13 for her mental examinations. The same day, he ordered Paula to the hospital for the same reason, and for an additional reason—to await childbirth.

Rabb had guessed Paula's condition the first time he saw her in court, and he was the first official to whom she admitted that she was pregnant. She gave birth to a girl the same day she went to the hospital, January 13. The baby was placed in a foster home by the Department of Public Welfare pending the outcome of the trial. Paula named her daughter Gertrude.

By the time the case came to trial, all the defendants had filed "suggestions of insanity," and psychiatrists had reported all to be mentally sound. On January 28, court-appointed doctors Dwight W. Schuster and Ronald H. Hull reported to Judge Rabb, in a letter, that Mrs. Baniszewski was mentally sound and able to stand trial. They added that she "appeared to be of average intelligence" and was, in their opinion, sane at the time of the crime.

Judge Rabb set Mrs. Baniszewski's long-delayed arraignment for 9:30 a.m. the following Thursday, February 3.

Meanwhile, Paula, recovered from childbirth, was arraigned and pleaded not guilty. She then was sent back to the hospital for the mental tests that had been postponed by the childbirth.

Coy Hubbard and Johnny Baniszewski had pleaded not guilty six days before, and Rabb had denied the motion to quash Johnny's indictment at that time. Jenny Likens attended the court session and cried when the court clerk read the indictment, setting out the charges against the six defendants.

On February 9, Dr. Hull and Dr. Dewitt W. Brown reported to Rabb, by letter, that they believed Richard Hobbs "is not psychotic, that he is of at least normal intelligence and that he is quite capable of cooperating in the preparation and execution of his defense."

The same two psychiatrists reported on Paula's condition a short time later. She was alert and perceptive, they said, and her "thought processes were well organized. . . . She showed characteristics of an immature, hysterical type personality, from an emotionally deprived background." But she was mentally competent, they said.

The doctors reported further that Paula denied injuring Sylvia, and "she represented the situation generally as one in which the girl Sylvia had become quite withdrawn and negativistic in her behavior to the extent that she would not eat and showed no response to pain." The doctors said Paula told them she did not believe Sylvia's condition was serious prior to her death.

Going further into Paula's emotional background, the doctors said Paula told them her parents, John and Gertrude Baniszewski, had a very poor relationship and she believed it was due to her father's mistreatment of her mother, a mistreatment repeated by Dennis Wright.

At a formal hearing March 16, in which the psychiatrists testified, Judge Rabb ruled that Mrs. Baniszewski, Paula Baniszewski and Richard Hobbs were mentally competent to stand trial. Coy Hubbard and Johnny Baniszewski would be examined later. At one of the hearings Stephanie, who had been drawing sketches of Judge Rabb and Jesus Christ during the proceedings, handed her attorney a note on which she had written, "I need a psychiatrist." But the matter never got much further than that with her.

Discouraged by the sanity reports and the outcome of other preliminary legal skirmishing, defense attorneys began to concentrate on the prosecution's insistence on trying all six defendants together. That seemed to defense attorneys the most vulnerable point of attack, from a legal standpoint.

The defense knew that if the state won all the preliminary legal battles, the defendants were in trouble. Going into trial, they would be faced by Leroy K. New, chief trial deputy in the Marion County Prosecutor's Office.

Suave and commanding in appearance, devastating in debate, ruthlessly effective on cross-examination, New had been chief trial deputy for several Republican prosecutors; he had sent several high state officials to prison for highway land-buying fraud; he had gained convictions of local vice kings who kept teenage prostitutes in slavery; and he had never lost a murder case. The closest he had come to losing a murder case was in the acquittal—by reason of temporary insanity—of a jail prisoner in the fatal beating of another inmate. But even then the prisoner's insanity was held likely to recur; and he was committed to a mental institution indefinitely, and for at least two years.

Tall, athletic, and handsome, about 40 years old, New possessed pointed facial features suggesting the blade of a hatchet; and his courtroom technique was just as cutting. A former professional saxophonist, he could play a jury as Paderewski played the piano.

So, partly in an effort to cut down on New's effectiveness and enthusiasm, defense attorneys began filing motions for separate trials for each defendant. Rice was first, with a motion for separate trial for Paula, on January 21. John Hammond soon followed, for Stephanie.

Their argument was that placing one defendant at the same table with the others, in the same trial, would hopelessly prejudice the jury against any one defendant. For instance, testimony against Gertrude Baniszewski might not be admissible against Johnny Baniszewski, and the jury would be instructed to disregard it when considering Johnny's guilt or innocence. But the jury would have heard the testimony, attorneys argued, and would have trouble putting it out of mind. Moreover, they argued generally, the mere charging of the children along with the evil Mrs. Baniszewski would cause the jury to associate them with her in their thinking, with prejudicial results.

Rabb took little time in denying the motion for separate trial for Stephanie, explaining that the law of Indiana prescribed joint trial when the defendants are charged with acting "in concert." Rarely, however, had so many been tried together on a murder charge; and the joint trial of five children on a murder charge was unprecedented.

Forrest Bowman, attorney for Johnny and Coy, pressed the issue. He filed a motion for separate trial for Johnny on February 7. Oral arguments on the motion were conducted before Rabb on March 30.

"It is bad enough," Bowman argued, "to require him to sit in court while his mother is being tried." But in addition, he said, the boy would be on trial himself, and he might find it necessary to testify in his own defense. Now some of this testimony, Bowman argued, might be harmful to his mother, so he might be reluctant to testify in his own defense.

"The state is saying to the boy, in effect," Bowman said, "send your mother to the electric chair or go yourself."

The county prosecutor's chief counsel, Frank E. Spencer, leaped to the floor in rebuttal. The law does not require separate trials, he noted; it was discretionary with the judge. And the circumstances of this case, he argued, required a joint trial.

"I wish to point out that this is a murder case," Spencer said. "The defendant and others are charged with murder. The law leaves it entirely within the discretion of the court as to whether there should be a separate trial. When several are charged with acting together in a murder, it is always best to present the whole thing at one time. The law contemplates it; the law allows it."

Leroy New explained the idea of joint trial later, outside the courtroom. When defendants are charged with committing a crime "in concert," he said, "the jury or judge couldn't get the total picture if only one person's part is told. Evidence against the others would be inadmissible."

This meant that with all being tried together, the jury could hear what all the defendants did, if anything, and judge the full impact of what each did. What one person did still would not be admissible against another person, but the jury could at least see the full meaning of the one person's act.

It would probably be hard to prove that what any one defendant did to Sylvia Likens was enough to kill her. But taking all their actions together, a murder case might be made. And defense attorneys then would have a harder time shifting the blame to other defendants, as physicians would testify that they could not be certain exactly which injury caused death.

Judge Rabb agreed with the deputy prosecutor; he denied Bowman's motion. Bowman sought to have that and other preliminary rulings overruled in the Indiana Supreme Court, but he was unsuccessful.

When it became apparent that Rabb would not lean over backward to help them, the defense attorneys began seeking to take the case outside his jurisdiction. Had they acted early enough on this strategy, they would have been successful, for Indiana law required a court to grant a change of venue from the county if the motion was filed within a specified time limit.

After the limit, though, granting the motion becomes discretionary. There will always be the question, however, of whether the lawyers actually wanted the change, or whether they merely wanted the judge to give them an adverse ruling so that they would have another point to raise on appeal later.

The first motion for change of venue was on March 1, for Johnny Baniszewski, by Ferdinand Samper, who was substituting for his vacationing junior law partner, Forrest Bowman. The motion said the defendants would not be able to get a fair jury in Marion County because of extensive newspaper, radio and television publicity on the case. Judge Rabb denied the motion for technical faults.

But he had had a conference with lawyers in the case in his chambers at the time the motion was filed, and that conference led to the first motion for change of judge. Stephanie's attorney, John Hammond, filed that motion, alleging that during the discussion in chambers, "much heated animosity appeared prevalent between Ferdinand Samper and the Honorable Saul I. Rabb," supposedly indicating Rabb was prejudiced. Hammond noted that Samper was Rabb's opponent in the coming primary election for the nomination of judge of Criminal Court, Division 2.

But he did not mention that Samper was merely substituting for Bowman and that he was not an attorney of record in the case. In another motion filed the next day, Deputy Prosecutor New pointed that out; and he added that he, too, had attended the discussion and had observed "no hostility between such persons" and that there had been no remarks "which were angry or unreasonable."

The following day, Rabb denied the motion for a change of judge, as he was to deny similar motions from then on. On March 29, he denied an amended motion by Bowman for change of venue.

But Rabb did agree to provide state funds for a psychiatrist to examine Johnny Baniszewski.

The last day of February, Judge Rabb announced that the Likens murder trial would begin on Monday, March 7. Bowman's motion for change of venue caused a postponement from that date, however. It appeared there might have to be a further postponement when a tuberculosis patch test on Johnny Baniszewski proved positive. A chest X-ray determined that he did not have TB, however.

Meanwhile, the usual voluminous motions being filed by William C. Erbecker, attorney for Mrs. Baniszewski, were causing delays of their own.

Judge Rabb denied Erbecker's motion to quash the indictment on February 3. So Erbecker moved for a continuance of Gertrude's arraignment for time to prepare a "plea in abatement," and the continuance was granted.

The arraignment was postponed again on February 9 as Erbecker filed his plea in abatement; a motion to force the state to produce statements, documents, writings, recordings and other material used in its investigation; a motion for inspection of the grand jury transcript, and a motion for examination of County Prosecutor Noble R. Pearcy to determine whether improper questions were put to Mrs. Baniszewski. "The defendant is at a loss to understand what she is charged with," the motion said.

The plea in abatement contended, among other things, that Mrs. Baniszewski had no lawyer during her grand jury testimony, that she had no stenographer to record the proceedings for her, that the grand jury was not qualified because of its attempt to resign earlier, and that the grand jurors were biased by news of the Likens murder.

The next day, the prosecution filed a "demurrer" to Erbecker's plea in abatement; and on February 11, Judge Rabb sustained the demurrer, nullifying Erbecker's plea.

Rabb ordered Mrs. Baniszewski to be arraigned the following Friday, February 18, at 3 p.m. She finally was arraigned at that time, pleading not guilty and not guilty by reason of insanity. Rabb indicated a desire to set the case for trial, but Erbecker said he had some more motions to file the first of the next week, including a motion for separate trial and a motion to suppress evidence.

Rabb eventually denied those motions, and on March 7 he set the case for trial beginning April 18.

On April 12, the Indiana Supreme Court declined to overrule Rabb's denial of a change of venue. Charges that undue publicity would prejudice potential jurors were without merit, deputy prosecutors had argued. Publicity was widespread throughout the state, they contended, and taking the case to another county would not change things.

The trial, then, was actually set to begin on Monday, April 18, with jury selection. Anticipating numerous juror dismissals by attorneys, Judge Rabb had ordered two extra panels of potential jurors to be summoned to his court that week. Indianapolis' two major newspapers and the two major news wire services made preparation for full-time staff coverage of the trial. A newspaper in Italy cabled the Associated Press requesting daily stories on the trial.

Judge Rabb ordered extra benches and chairs for members of the press. Television newsmen asked what photographic equipment would be permitted in the courtroom; Rabb ruled that no pictures, still or moving, could be taken in the courtroom while the judge or jury was inside. One of the city's four TV stations, WFBM, arranged for students from the city's John Herron School of Art to make sketches at the trial for showing to viewers. TV station WTTV later sent other artists to the trial. Newsman Bill Aylward of WISH television arranged to broadcast daily reports on the trial from the judges' library.

The library and courtroom were in the five-story West Wing of the City-County Building, on the opposite end of the building from Police Headquarters. The wing contained sixteen modern courtrooms, all alike, for the Criminal Court, the Circuit Court, the Superior Court, the Probate Court, and the civil divisions of the Municipal Court. The two divisions of the Criminal Court were on the second story. Lawyers, government workers, relatives of victim and defendants, neighbors, crime buffs and regular courthouse hangers-on would press for admission daily to the courtroom's fifty-seat gallery.

That the trial was the most talked-about, read-about news story of the time could be proven easily.

Twenty journalism students at an East Side high school were quizzed by their teacher on names in the news. Only four members of the class were able to identify the name of Roger D. Branigin as that of the governor of Indiana. But only two were *unable* to identify *Sylvia Likens* as the name of the victim of a sadistic torture slaying.

On April 16, 1966, two days before the trial was to begin, Deputy Prosecutor Leroy New announced that the state would seek the death penalty for all defendants.

12

A "NICE GIRL," A JURY, AND AN ANGRY YOUNG MAN

IT WAS to be daughter vs. mother and sister vs. sister in what Deputy Prosecutor Leroy New later called "the most diabolical case ever to come before a court or jury."

The famed New York trial lawyer Louis Nizer wrote that "the excitement, surprise and meaningfulness of a real court contest are incomparable and elude imagination." The Likens murder trial had all those elements and then some.

Nizer contended that fictional trial scenes, such as in the movies or on television, are usually incorrect or inadequate.

"In fictional court scenes," he wrote, "one sharp contradiction often breaks the witness, who then hysterically screams a confession. In real life the witness' fortitude in the face of exposure is as remarkable as a human body's resistance to incredible torment."

Cross-examination will leave the witness "no retreat" and compel him "to admit his error," Nizer wrote, "yet he continues to fight back and clutch for the remote chance that the tide will turn and he will not go under." But one witness actually did break down in the Likens murder trial, a real-life drama that possessed fictional qualities as well.

THE ATMOSPHERE was informal as the trial began at 9:30 a.m. Monday, April 18, like a convention that has yet to get into gear. Before jury selection could begin, Judge Saul Rabb had some unfinished business to attend to, including rulings to make on several motions filed just before the court closed the previous Friday.

Forrest Bowman had obtained his order for a psychiatric examination of Johnny Baniszewski, as a matter of defense, but he reported that he had been unable to find a psychiatrist willing to take the case, after diligent efforts. He petitioned the court for a postponement of the trial to give him more time to find one.

Bowman also had just assumed the case of Coy Hubbard, after Hubbard's first attorney, Joseph F. Quill, had withdrawn the previous week. So Bowman hastily filed for Hubbard motions similar to those he had filed earlier for Johnny, such as a motion for change of venue and a motion for separate trial. Rabb was faced also with new motions by Paula's attorney for separate trial and change of venue.

Gertrude's attorney, William Erbecker, asked for and received court funds with which to employ a defense psychiatrist to determine whether the woman "might be suffering from sadism or have propensities for sadistic acts."

Rabb's denial of Bowman's motion for a four-week continuance sent the young lawyer scurrying across town to the Statehouse again to ask the Indiana Supreme Court to force Rabb to grant the continuance. The Supreme Court unanimously turned down Bowman's bid for four weeks, but the hearing did delay the trial four hours.

The defendants had come prepared for a long trial. Stephanie, who was carrying two A's and two B's in her course work at the Juvenile Center, read a biology textbook as the attorneys questioned potential jurors and argued with the judge.

Gertrude, wearing a white blouse, sat stone still. Paula, in an old brown skirt and faded green blouse, slouched in her chair. She had observed her 18th birthday while awaiting trial.

Coy Hubbard, neatly attired in a gray suit, white shirt and tie, sat ramrod straight and attentive. Richard Hobbs, wearing a brown sport coat, hung his head in his hands. Johnny, wrapped in a blue windbreaker, fidgeted in his chair, his chin resting in his hand, his alert eyes focusing alternately on every corner of the courtroom. He had observed his 13th birthday in jail.

The defense lawyers were lined up at two long tables facing the jury box. Each defendant sat behind his own lawyer. Behind the defendants sat representatives of the press, lined against the wall.

To the right of the defense table, also facing the jury, was the prosecution table. Seated with Leroy New was the amiable Marjorie Wessner, a deputy prosecutor who had been selected to assist him in the case. In cases involving women and children defendants, the prosecutor's office liked to have a woman prosecutor to avoid giving the impression that New was bullying the defendants.

Seated behind New and Miss Wessner was Norman K. Collins, a prosecutor's investigator assigned to Criminal Court, Division 2. Behind Collins, at the front of the gallery, sat Sylvia Likens' surviving sisters, Jenny Likens, now 16, and Dianna Shoemaker, now 19.

Near them sat 10-year-old Shirley Baniszewski, a state's witness. Shirley was the subject of a slight altercation just before lunch between New and Collins, on the one side, and Stephanie's attorney, John Hammond, on the other. Hammond insisted that he was still Shirley's attorney, and he objected to her presence in the courtroom; he said he had not been informed that she had testified before the grand jury. The deputy prosecutors objected to her being allowed to talk to her mother.

Despite the confusion, New and Miss Wessner managed to tentatively accept twelve jurors before Bowman made his crosstown trip to the Supreme Court. New had asked potential jurors a brief series of questions regarding their ages, occupations, families, opinions, and feelings on the subject of capital punishment. At New's request, Judge Rabb excused one potential juror who said he had conscientious objections to capital punishment.

Things went much slower when the jury examination, called voir dire, was passed to Mrs. Baniszewski's lawyer, William Erbecker. He spent 45 minutes questioning the first juror and 20 minutes on the second before the court recessed for the day. Erbecker had already nettled Judge Rabb by returning to the court 45 minutes after the judge had called a 15-minute recess.

To each juror, Erbecker read a five-paragraph legal pleading he had filed in answer to the indictment. The pleading set out in detail Mrs. Baniszewski's plea of insanity. Erbecker reminded the jurors that it was the state's duty to prove Mrs. Baniszewski not only guilty beyond a reasonable doubt, but also to prove her sane beyond a reasonable doubt.

He asked the first juror whether he would expect a mother to have a greater degree of responsibility under the law than her children. "I would have to say yes," the potential juror said.

"Would you require less evidence against her, then?" asked the lawyer.

"No," he said. And so it went. "Are you going to hold her more culpable, more to blame than the minor children?" Erbecker asked the second juror.

Judge Rabb interceded: "Or would you require them to prove her guilty beyond reasonable doubt?"

"Sure," the juror replied.

"Sure," Rabb echoed. "Next question, please."

Three potential jurors questioned the first day expressed reservations about capital punishment but said they could go for it in certain circumstances.

The state's capital punishment law was at that time in abeyance. The 1965 legislature had repealed it, but the governor had vetoed the repeal, expressing a desire that the next legislature, in 1967, give it fuller consideration, and expressing a desire also that no one should die in the electric chair in the interim.

One potential juror had said he already considered Mrs. Baniszewski to be guilty, but he said he could listen to the evidence impartially and give her a fair trial. He was a teacher at Tech High School, where Sylvia and the elder Baniszewski girls had attended, but his only knowledge of the case was from reading newspapers, he said. He was later excused by attorney Bowman.

The courtroom was filled with spectators that first day, and it was to remain that way through seven tedious days of voir dire.

Erbecker held the floor throughout the second day, with a few brief questions interjected by New from time to time. Erbecker asked one potential juror, the brother of a state trooper, "Did you hear of this case before?"

"Of course," the man replied. He said he had no preconceived notions, however. But he was dismissed by the court later when he said he opposed capital punishment in principle.

Another man, excused for the same reason, had

remarked, "We on earth don't have a right to take life like that. The first death does not justify the second death."

Erbecker relinquished the floor to George Rice, attorney for Paula, late the third day, Wednesday, April 20.

The day had been marked by several incidents. Jenny Likens had been ushered from the gallery when she began crying during reading of the indictment to some newly arrived potential jurors. The gallery burst into applause later when a woman juror being questioned by Erbecker, in regard to Gertrude's sanity, remarked, "Some people just use insanity to try to get out of things."

Erbecker regarded the outburst as prejudicial to his client and asked Judge Rabb to dismiss all jurors who heard it, but Rabb refused.

Gertrude and her son Johnny kissed one another on the cheek before being led away by sheriff's deputies at the noon recess.

Erbecker had spent two days finding twelve acceptable jurors; Rice spent only a half-hour before adjournment Wednesday finding five acceptable jurors.

"Have you ever made any study of psychology, or criminology?" Rice asked the panel members. He wanted at least two people on the jury with knowledge of slum life.

Another of Rice's questions was, "Do you have a preference as to the Old Testament or the New Testament?" Later, the lawyer–professor explained, "I interpret a preference for the Old Testament to indicate a sense of vengeance and a preference for the New Testament as showing mercy."

John Hammond took over when Rice finished on Thursday. He asked jurors whether they agreed that premeditated malice, alleged in the indictment, meant that Stephanie "planned to kill Sylvia, and at a specified time."

But Deputy Prosecutor New, in later questioning, read from a law book that "malice may be implied from any deliberate act or cruel act" and that premeditation indicated a plan "to do something—not necessarily to kill—but to do something that results in death."

Many of the potential jurors said they would rather not serve on the jury, but they said they would serve willingly because it was their duty. One member of the regular jury panel, who had already served on four juries during that court term, said, "I would rather not be a juror, period—in the Likens case or any other case."

The lawyers "passed" a tentative jury of ten men and two women late Thursday. But there were still a number of "peremptory challenges" to be used, the privilege of excusing potential jurors without giving reasons. Twenty peremptory challenges were allotted to the state, and twenty to the defense.

Richard Hobbs' attorney, James G. Nedeff, had asked potential jurors whether they could be fair and unprejudiced even "if the evidence tends to prove lurid and shocking and horrid, and if pictures are introduced."

The attorneys did begin using their peremptory challenges more freely on Friday, April 22, and tempers flared for the first time in the trial. By the noon hour, New had become exasperated at Erbecker's tedious, repetitious questioning.

"We have sat by through a large extent of questioning," he told the judge, "which is probably irrelevant and not proper voir dire examination. When our objection to his question is sustained, Mr. Erbecker immediately goes back to the same line of questioning. It is an utter waste of time. I feel a comment is needed now, simply in the interest of getting this case over within the month. We'll be here forever."

Judge Rabb was wary of admonishing a defense attorney, for fear of giving him grounds for appeal, but he agreed with the deputy prosecutor that many of Erbecker's questions to jurors were "repetitious questions which may be detrimental to your client's interests. I am known throughout the state of Indiana, I think, as the most liberal judge on voir dire. But repetition is just pressing the point."

Many of Erbecker's questions had dealt with Mrs. Baniszewski's responsibility for what her children might have done. "Would you consider her mere presence as evidence of guilt?" was one question thrown out by Judge Rabb, after New objected. New contended that the purpose of voir dire was to find jurors who would follow the law and give a fair trial, without prejudice. The defense lawyer was not allowed to plead his case during voir dire, New argued.

"Am I being restricted, Your Honor?" Erbecker asked, attempting to lead the judge into an appealable error.

"You are not being restricted in any way," Rabb replied kindly.

At this point, Forrest Bowman renewed his motion for separate trial for his two clients. He said Erbecker's "badgering" of potential jurors would prejudice them against all defendants.

Friction became intense as Judge Rabb extended the normal 5 p.m. quitting time to past 7 p.m. in an effort to get a jury. Erbecker continued his line of questioning; New continued his objections, and Rabb continued to sustain New.

Erbecker asked to have the jury excused from the courtroom temporarily. The defense had ten peremptory challenges left, and Erbecker said he was using all ten of them to dismiss all but two of the tentatively accepted jurors, on grounds he was being restricted in voir dire.

Other defense lawyers leapt to their feet, objecting that Erbecker had no right to use all the challenges himself. Judge Rabb agreed with them and disallowed the blanket challenge, noting that Erbecker already had made most of the peremptory challenges used.

The jury was ushered back into the courtroom. "Do you have a motion to make?" the irritated judge asked Erbecker.

"No, Your Honor," answered the lawyer, fearing he would alienate the jurors if they knew he wanted to excuse ten of them. But Rabb restated the motion anyway, for the jurors to hear. Erbecker then withdrew the motion and asked for a mistrial, which was denied. The trial was recessed until the following Monday.

The parents of victim and accused showed up in the courtroom for the first time in the trial that Friday. Lester Likens, now 40, and Betty Likens, now 38, sat in front of the gallery, tanned from their resumed tour with the carnival in the Florida sun. They and their son Danny, now 19, had driven a broken-down truck to its death near Nashville, Tennessee, in an effort to get back to Indianapolis for the trial, and they pooled their final resources for bus fare the rest of the way to the city.

The other courtroom visitor was Mrs. Baniszewski's ex-husband, rock-jawed John S. Baniszewski Sr., 39 years old, father of three of the defendants. He lavished his attention on Stephanie, and to a lesser degree on Johnny. Stephanie cried when her father embraced her as he arrived in the courtroom at the end of the day.

Stephanie, carrying a paperback copy of the Gospel According to St. John, had a long noon-hour conversation that day with her attorney and Deputy Prosecutors New and Wessner. It was a prelude to the trial's most dramatic event so far, to occur the following Monday.

That Monday morning, April 25, as the first order of business, New offered to join in Stephanie's motion for a separate trial, saying the evidence justified it.

At the same time, the deputy prosecutor announced: "As of now, we have the expectation that she will testify for the State of Indiana. She has been called as a state's witness. But she doesn't have to testify, on a felony, and if she does, it will be completely voluntary."

Other lawyers immediately charged that there was a sellout. As events proved, the grand jury eventually reconsidered Stephanie's case and set her free with "no bill."

Other attorneys renewed their motions for separate trial, but to no avail. Judge Rabb granted Stephanie's, but only because the state had joined in it, he said.

New said he and Miss Wessner had decided Sunday to separate Stephanie from the other defendants after "we obtained substantial evidence over the weekend." He declined to discuss the evidence, but it pertained to Stephanie's attempts to rescue Sylvia and to her minor participation in torturing the girl.

Hammond, Stephanie's attorney, was jubilant. He knew he had won his part of the case before testimony even started. He had maintained all along that Stephanie was a "nice girl," who showed much promise. He was even prepared to introduce medical testimony that she was a virgin.

Jury selection continued in slow fashion that Monday, but attorneys agreed rapidly the next day on a jury of eight men and four women, all white, to hear the case. All but one were parents, most of them with children about Sylvia's age.

The jurors included a 39-year-old housewife; a 35-year-old General Motors Corporation machinist; a 23-year-old engineer who had known Sylvia Likens as a customer at his father's grocery store; a 58-year-old woman television survey pollster; a 36-year-old transportation agent for Trans World Airlines; a 47-year-old assistant sales manager for a manufacturing company; the 42-year-old wife of another General Motors employe; a 36-year-old General Motors mechanical engineer; a 39-year-old communications worker for the National Guard; the 45-year-old wife of an employe of Eli Lilly & Co., a pharmaceuticals manufacturer; a 59-year-old general foreman at the International Harvester company, and a 50-year-old laboratory technician at Eli Lilly.

Two women were selected as alternate jurors—one the wife of a General Motors employee, the other a divorcee and General Motors secretary.

In selecting the jury, the state had obtained the dismissal of fifteen potential jurors who expressed conscientious objections to capital punishment and eight potential alternates on the same grounds. The state used five peremptory challenges.

Erbecker, Mrs. Baniszewski's lawyer, obtained five dismissals by the court of potential jurors who showed prejudice, and he used nine peremptory challenges. Paula's lawyer, George Rice, obtained one court dismissal and used two peremptory challenges. John Hammond had used one peremptory challenge before Stephanie was removed from the trial. Forrest Bowman had used one peremptory for Johnny Baniszewski and one for Coy Hubbard. Richard Hobbs' attorney, James Nedeff, excused no jurors.

During the jury selection, buzzing around the scene with members of the press was a tall, lean, pipe-smoking youth with an Ivy League look. He was an angry and earnest young man from Wayne, New Jersey, and Antioch College in Yellow Springs, Ohio.

He identified himself to Judge Rabb and the attorneys as Jay Tuck, 20 years old, representative of the American Humanist Association and its collegiate organization, the Humanist Student Union of North America.

"There's something wrong here," Tuck told anyone who would listen. "Something very wrong—that something like this could happen."

He was talking about the trial of five teenagers on charges of first-degree murder, as well as about the torture slaying itself.

"I'm here to find out what's going on," Tuck told his listeners. He asked how the torture was allowed to happen. "I'd like to know where the police were, where the Welfare Department was, where others were who could help."

Tuck said he was interested also in the issue of capital punishment, "which we believe is wrong," and in the defendants' insanity pleas. If found insane, he asked, would the defendants be any better off in a mental Hospital than in prison?

The angry young humanist was concerned also

about the widespread publicity the case had received, and to which he was about to add, as associate editor of the *Humanist* magazine. "Everyone seems to have preconceived notions of the case," he complained.

True to form, defense attorney William C. Erbecker interviewed Jay Tuck as a possible defense witness for Gertrude Baniszewski. As things worked out, Erbecker called about everyone *but* Jay Tuck to the witness stand.

13

A SLUGGISH START

"THE EVIDENCE will show that Sylvia Marie Likens was born in Lebanon, Indiana, January 3, 1949, and was 16 on January 3, 1965. . . ."

Deputy Prosecutor Leroy K. New stood tall and erect, reading expressively but unemotionally from typewritten sheets of yellow, lined, legal-sized notebook paper. Spectators standing in the rear of the courtroom craned their necks to get a glimpse of one of the state's best trial lawyers as he read the prosecution's opening statement to the jury.

"The evidence will show," New continued, "that Jenny and Sylvia became acquainted with a neighbor girl on East New York Street, Naomi McGuire. You will see her sister, Darlene McGuire, who frequented the Baniszewski house until she was ordered by her parents not to return inside the house ever again. . . .

"The evidence will show that immediately after her parents left the house for the last time, Gertrude turned to Sylvia and said, 'What are you going to do now, Sylvia, now they're gone?' . . .

"The evidence will show that one time Gertrude picked up a knife, held it menacingly in her hand, approached Sylvia and told her to 'Come on . . . fight me back,' and Sylvia said she didn't know how to fight. The evidence will show that Sylvia received a cut completely through the jeans on one leg and on her wrist in that encounter. . . .

"The evidence will show that Sylvia suffered from malnutrition at the time of her death and Gertrude told a neighbor girl that she had seen Sylvia eating out of the garbage can. . . .

"The evidence will show that Gertrude and John and Paula planned to get rid of Sylvia by dumping her in a place called Jimmy's Woods the day before she died. . . .

"The evidence will show that she defecated and eliminated her bowels in her shorts in the basement and that she continued to moan. . . .

"The evidence will show that at no time was Sylvia taken to a doctor or given any medication except for alcohol or Merthiolate on the open burns. . . ."

New read for 45 minutes, his delivery commanding the attention of everyone in the courtroom throughout. His straightforward account was probably the most accurate, most complete, most horror-striking résumé of the crime up to that time.

Then came the defense's turn to summarize what it would prove. William C. Erbecker, 10 minutes late getting back from a recess that followed New's statement, took the floor after being gently reminded by Judge Rabb to be on time in the future.

"Gertrude Baniszewski has no opening statement as to what she will prove," Erbecker began.

"It is blatantly obvious," he shouted, quickening the pace, "that the State of Indiana has made a deal with one of the co-defendants."

New objected to this reference to Stephanie Baniszewski. "Sustained, as to the type of language," Judge Rabb said.

"The state's own evidence," Erbecker resumed, "will create a reasonable doubt in your mind as to how this death occurred." Erbecker finished in three minutes, having been cautioned again by Rabb to confine his statement to what he intended to prove.

Attorneys George P. Rice Jr. and Forrest B. Bowman Jr. waived their opening statements. Attorney James G. Nedeff took the floor for the defendant Richard D. Hobbs.

Nedeff promised that his client would take the stand and admit tattooing and branding Sylvia. Then the lawyer explained: "Richard Hobbs is guilty of some offense, but I can assure you he is not guilty of first-degree murder. At most, he is guilty of immaturity and gross lack of judgment."

After another five-minute recess, Erbecker moved for separation of defendants—meaning he wanted a separate table so that his client would not be associated with the "guilty" children—and a separation of witnesses, meaning that all witnesses but the one testifying must remain outside the courtroom.

Judge Rabb granted both motions. The idea of separation of witnesses is to keep their stories independent, to keep them from collaborating; it also meant that Sylvia Likens' grieving parents, who were to be witnesses, would be removed from the jury's sight. The state was allowed to keep one witness in the courtroom, however, and New and Miss Wessner chose Jenny Likens.

Testimony was to begin after lunch. Before it got under way, evidence was heard on Erbecker's motion to suppress testimony on remarks Gertrude had made to police.

"Did you effectively warn her of her constitutional right to remain silent?" he asked Patrolman Melvin Dixon.

"No, sir," he said. But he said he had no reason to suspect Gertrude at that time, as she attempted to implicate an anonymous gang of boys. Erbecker then put the same questions to another patrolman, Paul E. Harmon, and to Detective Sgt. Kaiser. Kaiser said he did not warn her of her rights when he first spoke with her because he did not suspect her. Later, he said, "I told her she didn't have to say anything, or do anything or sign anything until she had an attorney. She said she hadn't done anything wrong and she didn't need an attorney."

Erbecker asked about the mode of questioning, whether psychological pressure was used, and again asked Kaiser whether he had advised her of all her constitutional rights.

"I don't know what her constitutional rights are,"

the exasperated detective said. "The only thing I told her was she didn't have to say anything until she had an attorney."

Rice asked for a recess; Paula had to go to the restroom. The judge denied the request. "It's the hardest job I've got, to get everybody back together," he said, frustrated by attorneys turning 5-minute recesses into half-hour recesses.

Erbecker, who seized the opportunity to handle misdemeanor cases in Municipal Court during recesses, and Nedeff, who went home during the lunch hour for cat naps, were the worst offenders. When Rabb did grant a recess at the conclusion of Erbecker's questioning of Kaiser, he said to Rice, "You've always been here on time; I'll appoint you sergeant-at-arms to see everyone else is here."

Rabb overruled Erbecker's motion to suppress. He said that the United States Supreme Court case of *Escobedo* vs. *Illinois*, cited by Erbecker, did not apply in a case in which the defendant spoke to police voluntarily in an attempt to mislead them.

Finally, at 3 p.m., the state was able to call its first trial witness, Patrolman Dixon (all the testimony to this point had been on the motion to suppress). Dixon barely breathed his name before the four defense attorneys leapt to their feet with a new wave of constitutional objections. Bowman argued that Dixon should have had a search warrant to enter the Baniszewski house. Rabb overruled the objection; Dixon had been called there at the instance of Mrs. Baniszewski, and the door was wide open when he arrived.

New asked Dixon what Mrs. Baniszewski said. Attorneys for the four children objected; since the children were not present to hear Dixon's conversation with the woman, testimony about it would be hearsay as to them, and not admissible. Judge Rabb sustained the objection as to the children only; the jury was instructed to consider the ensuing testimony as to Gertrude only and to disregard it as to the children.

Such objections to testimony about conversations were to continue throughout the trial, and so were the confusing instructions to the jury. With five defendants on trial, there was almost certain to have been at least one of them missing during any given conversation.

Dixon testified about his talk with Gertrude, and then New introduced the first four gruesome pictures of Sylvia's body as it lay on the upstairs mattress.

The courtroom was engulfed in another flood of objections. "Dixon was not present when the photographs were taken. . . . He had no right to be there. . . . The pictures are inflammatory and prejudicial. . . ." But New elicited testimony that the pictures were "true and accurate representations" of what Dixon had seen, and that he had entered the house properly.

Rabb allowed the photographs to be passed to the jury at 3:36 p.m. The twelve men and women each took three or four seconds with each picture, viewing the girl's savagely battered body with grim but

unflinching faces. The woman juror in the fourth
seat hung her head after viewing the last of the four
photos.

New asked Dixon about the note Mrs. Baniszewski had given to him. The objections began all
over again. Judge Rabb told the jurors to disregard
the note except for the cases against Gertrude and
Paula, who were present when Dixon received the
note. New read the note aloud, in which Sylvia supposedly explained her torture by a gang of boys. The
note was then passed to the jury.

Little progress had been made the first day, with
nearly every question meeting a torrent of objections, many of them sustained or partially sustained.

The jury was sent home to return at 10:30 a.m.
the next day.

Before others went home, Johnny Baniszewski
made a brief appearance on the witness stand.
"What is your name and address?" asked his lawyer, Bowman.

"John Baniszewski, 3850 East New York Street,"
the boy snapped back.

"That's all," Bowman said, and the boy returned
to his seat, whispering to his lawyer, "How'd I do?"
It was his only appearance on the stand during the
trial, and the purpose was technical—to prove that it
was his house the patrolman had entered illegally.
The point did not score with Rabb, but Bowman had
another point to raise on appeal, if necessary.

14

THE DEFENDANTS FALL OUT

THURSDAY, APRIL 28, 1966, the second day of evidence. At the far left end of the defendants' dock, alone at a single table, sat William Erbecker, attorney for Gertrude Baniszewski. To his right, at a longer, slightly higher table, sat the three attorneys for the four other defendants. That's the way they wanted it. Erbecker was having nothing to do with the other lawyers, and they were having nothing to do with him. They were working at cross purposes.

Their trial on a common charge was all that was holding the five defendants together. Erbecker would paint Mrs. Baniszewski as a frail, distraught, insane woman who was unaware of tortures the children were inflicting on Sylvia or unable to stop them if she was aware (later, he changed his strategy to insanity alone). While Erbecker would be trying to push the blame onto the children, the children's lawyers would be trying to push it onto Gertrude or onto the other children, whoever could take the rap. It was like having four extra prosecutors in the courtroom.

But even with separate tables, the other attorneys felt they had a hard time demonstrating their split with Erbecker. His voluminous written pleadings were matched by his verbose courtroom rhetoric; and the jury, the other attorneys feared, might get the impression he was "chief" defense counsel. This was one point in their pleas for separate trials.

After a brief hearing in which the judge denied Bowman's motion to suppress Dixon's testimony, and after a brief cross-examination of Dixon by Erbecker, the state called its next witness, Patrolman Harmon.

He faced the same battery of questions from defense attorneys about search warrants and constitutional rights, but New did manage to get him to identify a number of objects brought into the courtroom in a large cardboard box—an iron anchor bolt; pieces of bent curtain rod; some orange-painted wooden slats; a three-inch-wide black leather belt; a quarter-inch-thick fraternity-style paddle; a pair of soiled girl's shorts.

Erbecker was 13 minutes late to the afternoon session. "I'm sorry, Your Honor," he panted as he rushed into the courtroom where the others were waiting.

Sgt. Kaiser took the stand. After another battery of preliminary questions by defense lawyers, he was allowed to answer the deputy prosecutors' questions for the benefit of the jury. He testified piecemeal, waiting for leading questions from New before going on. Defense attorneys objected that this served to unduly emphasize his testimony. Judge Rabb asked him several times to relate the whole story of his investigation in one monologue.

At one point in the monologue, Erbecker objected that Kaiser had failed to advise Gertrude of her rights, saying she was "nervous and excited, under fear, and of unsound mind." That brought a ripple of laughter from the gallery, whereupon Erbecker moved for declaration of a mistrial "because of the emotional outburst of the spectators."

Rabb denied the motion, but that did not keep the lawyer from moving for mistrial a number of subsequent times during the trial. Erbecker continued his harangue that Kaiser had subjected Gertrude to "duress, fraud and coercion . . . unlawfully and illegally detained the defendant when he did not know her constitutional rights . . . she was held in the police department without food, sleep or rest and had no attorney."

"Objection overruled," said the judge calmly.

Kaiser continued to relate his conversation with Gertrude.

During a midafternoon recess, Erbecker again took up his cudgel against the police department. "He knew she had an attorney," the lawyer said of Sgt. Kaiser. "She's entitled to counsel. This is in the category of an inquisition." He appealed to the *Escobedo* decision and the case of *Gideon* vs. *Wainwright*.

"I have read both *Escobedo* and *Gideon* many a time," the judge informed the lawyer. Pointing out that he had already denied Erbecker's motion to suppress, the judge continued, "Constant repetition does not make your point any stronger. The circumstances of the facts when a person calls the police and gives them a note are much, much different. I don't think *Escobedo* says every policeman has to carry a lawyer around in his back pocket." (Erbecker was to laugh up his sleeve a few weeks later when the United States Supreme Court ruled, in *Miranda* vs. *Arizona* and other cases, in effect, that if a policeman does not have a lawyer in his pocket, he had better know where to call one before questioning a suspect.)

Finished relating Gertrude's denials of harming Sylvia, Kaiser proceeded to Richard Hobbs' written statement. Attorneys for the other defendants spent the rest of the day arguing that parts relating to their clients should be deleted before the statement was read to the jury. But Hobbs' attorney, James Nedeff, objected to taking any part of the statement out of context. The jury had been sent home for the day. Rabb took the objections under advisement and ruled the next day that the statement should be read in full. But he admonished the jury to consider it as to the case against Hobbs only.

Jenny Likens, who had stayed home sick the last two days, was back in the courtroom on Friday, April 29. She sat behind the prosecutor's table, coughing deeply at intervals, shifting her large, sad eyes from witness to defendants and back again. She wore her dingy blond hair in a long ponytail, and a faded orange cotton dress, white socks and red oxfords, one of which was permanently affixed to her brace.

Before Sgt. Kaiser was recalled to the witness stand, Rabb heard from psychiatrists who had examined Coy Hubbard and Johnny Baniszewski the day before. He ruled the two boys mentally competent to stand trial.

The jury was ushered into the courtroom, and Kaiser returned to the stand. Leroy New read Hobbs' signed confession to the jury. Ricky hung his head and covered his ears. The other defendants sat impassive.

"Do you have an opinion as to whether Mrs. Baniszewski was sane or insane when you talked to her?" New asked the detective at the close of his testimony.

"Yes," he said. Erbecker's objection was overruled.

"What is that opinion?"

"She was sane." New relinquished his witness to the defense for cross-examination.

Erbecker made little progress on the familiar theme of Gertrude's "violated" rights. Meanwhile, Rabb ordered the standing spectators to leave the courtroom. "There is too much moving around, too much whispering," he said.

Erbecker got Kaiser to list his vast experience as a policeman, then reminded him of the sadistic details of the crime. "Do you still say," he asked incredulously, "she is a sane and normal person?"

The detective reaffirmed his opinion. Other attorneys asked him few questions, and Deputy Coroner Dr. Arthur Paul Kebel was next to take the stand after a 15-minute recess.

Kebel related his discovery that Sylvia's body, when he first saw it, "was surprisingly clean compared to the other surroundings in the room."

New asked him to relate evidence he found of physical injury.

"Well," the doctor gasped, "I hardly know where to begin."

Defense attorneys' objections to that remark were sustained.

Kebel related what he saw in gory detail, holding the jurors 11 minutes past their usual lunch recess time.

"In your opinion," asked Deputy Prosecutor New as he finished his questioning of the deputy coroner after lunch, "was Gertrude Baniszewski sane or insane?"

"I would say she was a sane person at that time."

But Erbecker saw an opportunity and seized it on cross-examination. Showing the doctor a photograph of Sylvia's mangled body on the slab at the city morgue, he asked: "Have you ever, in all your experience, seen such a sight as that?" Defense attorney Bowman objected and was sustained.

But Erbecker pursued the matter. In a lengthy hypothetical question, running hundreds of words, he detailed for Kebel the evidence that was in so far—of the fantastic injuries the girl had suffered. "Is it still the belief on your part," he asked, "that Gertrude Baniszewski was of sound mind?"

Kebel explained that when he saw the body, he had no reason to connect Gertrude with the crime. But as for the body's mutilation itself, he said, "I thought it was the work of a madman."

Knowing the doctor's penchant for glowing in the limelight of the witness stand, Erbecker pressed him further, asking him whether he believed the murderer suffered from sadism. Resisting efforts by the judge and other attorneys to make him answer yes or no, Kebel said, "I think your question should be answered by a psychiatrist." But he indicated a desire to express an opinion of some sort, and a rephrased question by Erbecker brought this reply: "I would say that only a person completely out of contact with reality would inflict this kind of agony on a human being."

Bowman, offended by Erbecker's style of questioning, asked that the jury be instructed to disregard it as to his own clients, Johnny Baniszewski and Coy Hubbard. "It puts them in the position of being prosecuted by Mr. Erbecker," Bowman complained, "or represented by him, and either way it would deny them their choice of counsel." The objection was overruled.

The pathologist, Dr. Charles R. Ellis, took the witness stand. New offered into evidence the ghastly photographs taken of the body at the autopsy, showing the girl's completely naked body with all its wounds. The blown-up pictures, visible to almost everyone in the courtroom, were first passed down the line of defense lawyers for possible objections. As they passed near Jenny Likens, she covered her eyes. As the lawyers argued over introduction of the photos, she began to cough and cry. She was led from the courtroom by investigator Norman Collins.

Before allowing the pictures to be shown to the jury, Judge Rabb admonished the jurors not to be inflamed by them. "They are not in evidence for that purpose," he said.

Later, as Dr. Ellis described the injuries he found, Jenny re-entered the courtroom, having composed herself. She sat through the rest of the day's session with a determined look on her face.

Propped on an easel before the jury were two large outlines of the human body, one for the front and one for the back of the body. As Ellis testified, he used three colored pencils to sketch in different types of wounds, marking them in where he had found them on Sylvia's body. By the time he finished, the diagrams were motley combinations of red, green and purple.

After a day of sordid testimony, the jury was due for a rest. Court was recessed until 9:30 a.m. on Monday, May 2.

15

STAR WITNESS

CROSS-EXAMINATION OF Dr. Ellis by defense attorney Erbecker the following Monday served only to add a few more details to the picture of Sylvia's agonizing death, to add a few more colorations to the diagrams on the easel. So the lawyer made another desperate attempt to convince the jury that Gertrude Baniszewski was insane.

"Do you agree with Dr. Kebel that it was the work of a madman completely out of touch with reality?" he asked. Objection, sustained.

So Erbecker established that the doctor had taken courses in abnormal psychology, in order to qualify him for an opinion on sanity, and launched into a longer hypothetical question than he had posed to Dr. Kebel. "Assuming all those facts in evidence," he concluded after several minutes, "could you state an opinion as to her sanity?" Objections by the state and by other defense attorneys were sustained. Dr. Ellis had never talked to Gertrude Baniszewski.

After the jury left the room for a half-hour recess,

defense attorney Bowman moved for a mistrial on the basis of Erbecker's long question. Its only purpose, he argued, was to restate to the jury evidence which had been ruled inadmissible as to the children. The motion was denied.

When the jury returned, Erbecker rephrased his hypothetical question numerous times, always meeting with objections, sustained. After more than a half-hour of this futile pursuit, he gave up. The court recessed for lunch.

Under cross-examination by Bowman after lunch, Dr. Ellis went into a minute description of the subdural hematoma (head injury) which he had listed as the principal cause of death. Was there any way to say which blow caused the internal bleeding?

"You could not say with certainty, especially in this case," the pathologist said. Under further cross-examination later by Richard Hobbs' attorney, James Nedeff, Dr. Ellis said something Bowman had wanted to hear but had been afraid to ask for. The bruise on the head, he said, was too big to have been caused by a broom handle. That seemed to absolve one of Bowman's clients, Coy Hubbard, of having struck the fatal blow.

But the bruise could have been caused by a fist, a board, a book, a fall down the stairs, a judo chop, a Coke bottle or a banging against the wall, Dr. Ellis said.

The doctor held to his opinion that the head injury was the ultimate cause of death, with the numerous other injuries, the shock and the malnutrition being contributing factors. "Given in time," he added, "medical treatment very well could have helped this patient."

At 2:30 p.m. the pathologist was permitted to return to his practice at Methodist Hospital. After a short recess the victim's father was sworn in as the next witness.

Deputy Prosecutor New guided Lester Likens through a recounting of Sylvia's life, and of his own often inadequate attempts to provide for her and the other children. New handed him a photograph: "Is that the house you lived in on Leland Street?"

Nostalgia swept the genial concessionaire's face. "I reckon that's so," he said. "It sure is."

Likens told of Mrs. Baniszewski's offer to care for his daughters and of the moment three months later when he learned of Sylvia's death. New handed him two more pictures, of his daughter's body on the slab at the city morgue in Marion County General Hospital. "Objection," shouted Erbecker. "The sole purpose of this is to inflame and prejudice the jury."

"—To elicit an emotional response in front of the jury," chorused Forrest Bowman. "There is no reason to do that."

The reason, New argued, was for legally positive identification of the victim as Sylvia Likens, the witness' daughter.

Judge Rabb ruled that one picture would be sufficient for that, and he ordered that the more offensive of the two be withheld. Bowman renewed his objection. In reply, New quoted the Indiana Supreme Court: "A murderer cannot complain of the mess he makes just because it's gruesome."

The jury was out of the courtroom during this argument, and the pictures had been held face down. Bowman asked that the one picture be shown to Likens before the jury returned so that "a purely unnecessary scene will be avoided, I hope."

New, angry now, said he did not expect a "scene." The witness had seen the pictures before he came into the courtroom, he said. "We run our case," New complained to the judge, "and Mr. Bowman does not."

The jury returned; the picture was turned face up. Was that Lester Likens' daughter Sylvia? "Yes, sir," he said, choking back tears. He covered his eyes and rested his forehead on his left palm. New had no further questions.

On cross-examination, defense attorneys browbeat Likens for his failure to investigate Mrs. Baniszewski and her house, and for his shortcomings as a father. "Isn't it a fact," sneered Erbecker, "that in your moving from place to place, your family life and environment wasn't conducive to a wholesome atmosphere for all your children, was it?"

A familiar defense technique is to "put the victim on trial," to show that the victim invited death in some manner, thereby reducing the guilt of the defendant. In this case, the defense lawyers were putting the victim's parents on trial, so to speak. But if they were guilty of negligence, did that help convince the jury that poor Sylvia had her ghastly death coming to her?

Erbecker had questioned the truth of Likens' contention that he paid Gertrude $20 a week for his daughters' care. So when Erbecker finished his questioning, New introduced money order receipts totaling $220, and Likens had testified to making at least $80 in cash payments in person. The $300 total averaged out more than $20 a week.

The next day was primary election day in Indiana; there was no court session. In the race for the Republican nomination for judge of Marion Criminal Court, Division 2, Judge Saul I. Rabb crushed his only opponent, Forrest B. Bowman Jr.'s law partner Ferdinand Samper, 46,710 votes to 3,974.

Sylvia's mother, 38-year-old Betty Likens, was the first witness Wednesday morning. The portly woman, wearing a blue knit dress, was soft-spoken and slow to respond to questions. She related a few tidbits of her daughters' personal lives, but most of her testimony was repetitious of her husband's.

Police Sgt. Don R. Campbell followed, with Coy Hubbard's signed confession. The usual arguments about the "coerced confession" were raised by the boy's attorney, Bowman. In an intermission hearing out of the presence of the jury, the boy's mother, Virginia Hubbard, testified that she was called at work about 2 p.m. on October 27, 1965, and notified of her son's arrest. She said she rushed to police headquarters and "I asked them to let me see my son." She said she saw him briefly and "I asked to speak to them; they won't let me speak to them." The boy, being held only on a delinquency charge when questioned about the murder, had indicated that he did not want to talk to his parents.

Judge Rabb allowed the statement to be read to the jury, and Hubbard sat through the reading soberly, erect and nearly expressionless as usual.

Campbell testified that he talked to Hubbard for two hours and wrote down everything the boy said on the signed statement. The statement contained only 1½ typewritten pages. "Would it take you two hours to type a page-and-a-half?" Bowman asked. The policeman said yes. Bowman seemed not satisfied that everything was on there. "I'll ask you," he said, "if it isn't a fact he told you Gertrude Wright hit that girl in the head with a broom and he took it from her and broke it up so she could not do that." Campbell never answered that question; Erbecker objected and was sustained.

After the lunch recess came the witness everyone had been waiting for. Her appearance had been foretold in a prominent article in the city's morning paper, the *Star*. Tiny Jenny Likens hobbled gingerly to the witness stand.

For the first time in the trial, Deputy Prosecutor Marjorie Wessner conducted the questioning. "State your name to the court and jury," she said, smiling.

"Jenny Fay Likens," came the reply in a loud, clear voice.

The girl spoke in a casual, matter-of-fact manner as she related all she knew of the torture that led to her sister's death. The dramatic part of her testimony was to come the next day.

There was a brief question as to Jenny's credibility. When Miss Wessner asked her whether she had seen Mrs. Baniszewski wield a knife, Jenny responded, "They must have done a lot of this while I wasn't around, because I didn't see all that." Defense attorneys got considerable play out of that remark, asking how much of Jenny's testimony was merely repetition of stories she had heard.

At the close of the day's session, the jury took a trip on a sheriff's bus to 3850 East New York Street to view the scene of the crime. The Baniszewski half of the old gray double was vacant, and had been since the discovery of the murder. Magazines and school papers littered the upstairs floors. The furniture had been removed, but the mattress on which Sylvia died still rested on the floor of the back bedroom. In the basement was the coal shovel Mrs. Vermillion had heard the night of October 26; in the basement sink were cinders, remnants of the fire that had heated the makeshift branding iron used on Sylvia's stomach.

Freshly attired in a red and white checked blouse and gray jumper, Jenny resumed her direct testimony the next morning, in the same brave, straightforward manner, except that her composure slipped when she told the jury how Sylvia had said to her, "Jenny, I know you don't want me to die, but I'm going to die. . . ." Jenny broke into sobs for the first time in her testimony, and Judge Rabb granted a half-hour recess.

The girl finished her direct testimony before 11:30 a.m., maintaining her composure even when replying to Miss Wessner's last question, asking why she had not gone for help for her sister.

"I was scared," Jenny said quietly. "Gertrude just kept beating me. I guess I just did what she said—and I wish I didn't."

Defense attorneys did not let Jenny's negligence go at that. Finished "trying" the victim's parents, they put her sister on trial.

Mrs. Baniszewski's attorney, Erbecker, began by trying to show that Jenny was biased and had been coached in her testimony by the deputy prosecutors.

"You have a feeling of hatred for Mrs. Baniszewski, don't you?" the lawyer asked.

"I sure do," the girl replied, glaring at the woman.

"You would say or do anything to see her found guilty here, wouldn't you?"

"Yes—but not unless it was true."

In response to further questioning, she admitted she had gone over her testimony with New and Miss Wessner the day before. "But," she said, "all anybody ever told me to do was to tell the truth."

Erbecker hit at the theme of the alleged "deal" with Stephanie. Jenny said she knew more about what Stephanie had done than she had testified about. "What did you leave out?" Erbecker asked.

New objected, and was sustained. Stephanie was not on trial. After Erbecker tried several more times, New asked that the jury be excused momentarily; and he asked the judge to admonish Erbecker.

Judge Rabb did not want to have to admonish anyone, but he did ask the lawyer to "refrain from objectionable questions."

Erbecker moved for a mistrial on the basis of New's request, and was denied. He made another motion for mistrial later in the day when he learned that a juror had been in a courthouse elevator in which Stephanie's lawyer, John Hammond, was making sarcastic remarks about Erbecker. Bowman also had stepped onto the elevator, and Hammond goaded him, "Is Erbecker still cross-examining? Why don't you get a separate trial and get out of there like I did?"

Judge Rabb overruled the motion for mistrial, but he again admonished the jurors, when they returned to the courtroom, not to be influenced by remarks made outside the courtroom.

The wretched Jenny was brought to tears again in the afternoon as Erbecker and other lawyers battered her with questions of why she failed to help her sister.

"You were perfectly free to go and tell anybody you saw, weren't you?" asked Erbecker.

"Yes," said Jenny.

"You could've told neighbors about this if you wanted to, couldn't you?" he continued.

"I could've," she answered, her voice breaking. "That don't mean *I* wanted to die, though." She wiped tears away with her sleeve.

"But you didn't, did you, Miss Likens?"

"No."

Forrest Bowman, attorney for Coy and Johnny, came to Jenny's rescue. Seeking to throw the blame onto the mother, Bowman asked Jenny: "Were you afraid of Gertrude Wright?"

"Yes," she said.

"Was it your fear of Gertrude Wright that prevented you from telling anyone what happened to your sister?" Bowman asked.

"Yes," the girl sighed.

But then James Nedeff, attorney for Richard Hobbs, took over and bore down once more. "Who would have done anything in the world to you if you had said one word?" he asked. An objection to the question was sustained, but he persisted.

"Why didn't you go to a policeman?" he asked.

"Gertrude threatened me that if I told anyone," Jenny said, "I'd get the same treatment."

"Why didn't you ask your sister Dianna?" asked Nedeff.

"I didn't see her then," said Jenny.

"Why didn't you call your grandmother, your grandfather?"

Jenny, brushing away a tear, did not answer.

"Did you know Lester Leak, a guard at Brookside Park?" Nedeff persisted. "Why didn't you tell him your sister was sick?"

Jenny bit her lip. Nedeff asked her why she had not told John Baniszewski Sr. when he brought the police dog on October 23. Jenny wiped her tears away with her sleeve, not having been given a chance to explain that she had never even been introduced to Baniszewski and that he had never even come inside his ex-wife's home.

"Your sister was moaning in agony," Nedeff insisted. "Why didn't you tell him?"

The dam broke, and Jenny's tears gushed forth. "I told you why I didn't tell," she sobbed. Court was recessed for the day. As the lawyers and defendants left the room, Jenny's bent-over head still lay buried in her arm.

16

THE STATE RESTS ITS CASE

CROSS-EXAMINATION CONTINUED the morning of Friday, May 6. Erbecker delved into the teenage party the Likens children had thrown in California.

Jenny admitted telling Mrs. Baniszewski about the party. "Did you tell her it was a sex party?" the lawyer asked.

"I didn't tell her—we had a party, but I don't know about sex."

As Mrs. Baniszewski's lawyer pressed for details, Jenny hung her head, either in shame or from humiliation at Erbecker's insinuating questions. Most of the questions went unanswered, as Judge Rabb sustained objections that they were irrelevant. Finally, after a grueling total of nearly two days on the witness stand, Jenny was allowed to step down.

Next, Sgt. Leo Gentry, of the Police Department's juvenile branch, was called on for introduction of the signed confessions of Paula and Johnny Baniszewski. Attorneys objected strenuously that they were juveniles being held on juvenile delinquency charges and that use of the statements later in a murder trial against them violated their rights. Even Gentry admitted he thought he was questioning them for the possibility of filing delinquency charges.

Judge Rabb cited an Indiana statute permitting introduction of such evidence. "What do you think of *9-1607 Burns*, Mr. Bowman?" the judge asked Johnny's lawyer.

"I think it's probably fatally at variance with the Constitutions of the United States and of the State of Indiana," the young lawyer said.

"It's been up to the Supreme Court about 100 times, hasn't it?" the judge asked.

"Not since *Escobedo*," the lawyer answered. But Rabb overruled the objection.

Meanwhile, Erbecker was filing a written motion for mistrial, or, in the alternative, for a poll of the jury to determine prejudice. Supplemented with what the lawyer believed to be prejudicial newspaper accounts of the trial, the motion also cited the noise of spectators' "hissing," "jeering," and "buffoonery." The gallery, Erbecker said, was "a Roman arena here where they can wait for the kill."

Rabb, who had ordered standing spectators out of the courtroom several times for whispering, said he had not heard the noises cited by Erbecker. "The Constitution requires a public trial," he added.

Deputy Prosecutor New noticed that one of the articles tabbed as prejudicial was headlined, "8 Men and 4 Women Put on Jury in Likens Case." The deputy prosecutor was losing his patience with Erbecker. To label such an article prejudicial, New said, "seems like buffoonery itself."

Rabb reminded Erbecker that the jury was being instructed each time it left the courtroom not to read newspaper accounts of the trial and not to listen to broadcasts about the trial.

The legal arguments took the rest of the morning. When participants returned from lunch, there were a few empty seats in the courtroom gallery for the first time since testimony began. They were filled soon, and the trial had a standing-room-only audience the rest of the way. The spectators ranged from high school pupils to elderly women; many of the latter arrived an hour early each morning carrying sack lunches. One morning a woman was injured scrambling with another woman for a seat and needed hospital treatment.

As the afternoon session began, New read the statements of Paula and Johnny to the jury. On cross-examination by Bowman, Sgt. Gentry was caught in a slight slipup. He admitted that he did not offer to call Johnny's father before questioning the 12-year-old boy. He said he "had no idea where his father lived at all." So Bowman introduced an official police paper Gentry had had at the time of questioning that listed the father's name, age and address.

Mrs. Vermillion, the uncurious neighbor, was the next witness. She told about her two trips to the

Baniszewski house and about the scraping sound. On cross-examination she admitted that she had not called authorities with her information until April 25, 1966, six months after the murder and a week after the start of the trial. She said she called because she had seen a picture of Coy Hubbard in a newspaper identifying him as Paula's boyfriend. She said she knew that Paula's boyfriend was someone other than Hubbard, and she wanted to advise the prosecutor of the mistake.

Mrs. Vermillion told Erbecker she was not a prejudiced witness against Gertrude Baniszewski. "I felt sorry for the lady," Mrs. Vermillion said. "I felt she was a hard-working lady . . . all those kids to take care of."

Late in the afternoon, at the end of a harrowing week, deputy prosecutors felt they had time for one more witness. Ten-year-old Shirley Baniszewski was led into the courtroom by her foster mother and her lawyer, John Hammond. Wearing a school dress and carrying a small leather purse, the pretty little brunette took the stand smiling, promising to tell the truth.

She was asked to point out her mother in the courtroom, for legal identification. The sweet smile rapidly drooped into a frown, and the little girl was in tears as she pointed to Gertrude Baniszewski. Gertrude herself jerked her head to one side and covered her eyes, crying. Paula also cried as she was pointed out by her little sister.

Erbecker requested permission to ask some preliminary questions in the absence of the jury. Rabb sent the jury home until 9:30 a.m. the next Monday.

"Now, young lady," the lawyer began. He asked her a number of questions to determine whether she knew what it meant to tell the truth. Shirley said, "I know I should tell the truth," and she began crying again. Leroy New jumped to the floor and said he would object "if the questions are designed for interference with justice."

Shirley said she had failed the first grade, and Erbecker sought further to question her intelligence and competence. "Do you know how to spell Baniszewski?" he asked. She rattled it off, letter perfect.

"Do you know how to pronounce it?" the judge asked the girl.

"Ban-i-SHEF-ski," the girl said carefully. Erbecker had been mispronouncing it "Ban-i-ZOO-ski" throughout the trial.

Rested over the weekend, Shirley wore a large white bow in her hair Monday morning when she returned to the witness stand, and she was bright and perky. She told of Coy Hubbard's ramming Sylvia against the wall and smacking her. "And you were there?" asked Deputy Prosecutor Marjorie Wessner.

"Yeh," Shirley said, bouncing and smiling. The import of her words apparently was not within her grasp.

Shirley told of numerous atrocities she had witnessed and, in some cases, helped perform. "Was Sylvia a good girl?" asked Miss Wessner.

"She was helpful," Shirley said in a sweet voice that sounded sincere. "She'd help everybody in the house."

Why, she was asked on cross-examination, had she not said anything to anyone about the beatings? Didn't she ever talk to other children in the neighborhood?

"I played with them," Shirley said, "but I didn't tell them what was going on because I just thought they were punishing her."

Judy Duke, who had testified at the habeas corpus hearing, was the next witness. She testified, among other things, that Coy Hubbard had rubbed salt into Sylvia's sores, along with Paula. On cross-examination Bowman, Hubbard's lawyer, introduced Judy's signed police statement, which carried no mention of Hubbard's applying salt. No one else had testified to seeing Hubbard apply salt, either.

As in the habeas corpus hearing earlier, this slowly responding witness forced attorneys to be precise in their questions. George Rice, Paula's attorney, asked Judy about the "package of salt."

"It wasn't a package," the girl said.

"Box, then," said Rice.

"Yeh," Judy said, "a box." And then she answered Rice's question.

The state's most fantastic witness, 12-year-old Randy Lepper, followed Judy in the afternoon. His witness-stand mannerisms shocked and amused lawyers and spectators. Erbecker had introduced a motion that the boy undergo psychiatric examination to test his competence as a witness. Erbecker filed the same motion for a number of juvenile witnesses, and Rabb ruled that such examination was neither proper nor necessary.

Randy wore a tie and a bright red blazer; a shock of hair from his modified Beatle haircut hung nearly to his eyes. The impish smile from his cherubic face found its way across the courtroom if perhaps his soft, hoarse voice did not. He smiled, squirmed and fidgeted, occasionally rolling or flicking his eyes toward the ceiling as attorneys asked him questions.

What did Sylvia say when Randy and the others hit her? "She said ouch," he grinned, flicking his eyes upward. Gertrude drooped her head in her hand as he testified.

Randy told of Johnny's hosing off Sylvia on the basement floor shortly before Sylvia died. "Whose hose was he using?" asked Miss Wessner.

There was a long pause. Randy raised his eyes to the ceiling, then brought them down again. "Mine," he smiled.

To Erbecker's pleasure, Randy described Gertrude as "nervous." How could he tell? "Because my mom's got eleven children, and I can tell."

Had Randy ever seen Sylvia doing anything "unusual" in the Baniszewski house?

"I seen her studying a few times," he said.

Barbara Sanders, the public health nurse, was next to the stand, to tell about her October visit to the Baniszewski home. Not unexpectedly she was blamed by defense attorneys for having allowed the murder to occur.

Erbecker asked incredulously about Mrs. Baniszewski's story to the nurse that 16-year-old Sylvia had been kicked out of the house and her present whereabouts were unknown. "Did you check her story out?"

"No, sir," the nurse replied; "I had nowhere to go from there. . . ."

"Well," she admitted after another question, "it *was* a little out of the ordinary."

"What did you do about it?" asked Erbecker.

"I wrote it up," she said.

Explaining further, Mrs. Sanders said, "It was an anonymous complaint, which I receive many of. . . . I hear many more tales than you'd ever dream of. . . . It wasn't any more incredible than stories I hear every day, sir." She said she did not feel the case warranted any further investigation at that time; so she wrote her report on a "one time only" card.

The Baniszewskis' fundamentalist minister, the Rev. Roy Julian, was the state's next witness, telling of his visits to the home and the things he had overheard at church. He was followed by Grace Sargent, the woman to whom Paula had bragged on the church bus about breaking her wrist on Sylvia's jaw. When Paula said she had tried to kill Sylvia, did Mrs. Sargent believe it? "I really don't know what I did believe," the woman replied. "That's the burden of guilt I have."

It was 4:55 p.m. and time to adjourn. Leroy New announced that the state would rest its case the next morning, on the sixteenth day of trial.

The only state's witness that morning was Police Sgt. Don R. Campbell, already a witness earlier but recalled to testify on the sanity of Coy Hubbard, for whom a suggestion of insanity had been filed. "I'd say he was sane," the policeman said.

"Do you know how to interpret a thematic apperception test?" asked Hubbard's lawyer, Forrest Bowman. Campbell was no psychiatrist, but his testimony was the only evidence one way or the other on Hubbard's mental condition. Bowman later withdrew the suggestions of insanity for both Hubbard and Johnny Baniszewski.

It now was the defense's day in court, and the defendants were dressed for it. For the first time in the trial, Johnny wore a coat and tie. Gertrude wore a new, sleeveless, dark blue sweater.

The usual motions for directed verdict of acquittal and other similar motions by defense attorneys were quickly denied by Judge Rabb. Meanwhile, Erbecker was hurriedly serving subpoenas on newsmen and bailiffs for testimony on the mental and physical condition of Mrs. Baniszewski, whose case would be presented first.

The first defense witness thus turned out to be the author of this book, John Dean, a reporter for the *Indianapolis Star*, at that time covering the Likens trial.

Erbecker drew out my professional background, established how long I had been working on the case, and then asked whether I had an opinion on Gertrude's sanity. I said I did. Erbecker asked me to state that opinion; but the deputy prosecutor, New, objected, and Judge Rabb sustained the objection on grounds that I was not competent to testify on Mrs. Baniszewski's sanity. (It was not because I was not a psychiatrist or a psychologist; it was because I had never spoken with Mrs. Baniszewski.)

Had I been permitted to testify, I would have expressed the opinion that Gertrude Baniszewski was sane. However, Erbecker probably expected New to object. His motive was to create the impression with the jury that he had a newspaper reporter as a defense witness ready to testify that the woman was insane.

I had never told either Erbecker or New whether I thought Gertrude was sane or insane. New told me later that he suspected I believed her to be sane. But he said he objected to my testimony because he did not want a precedent established for calling newsmen as sanity witnesses. Although Erbecker had most other newsmen at the trial under subpoena, I was the only one he called.

His next witness was attorney John Hammond, by whom he hoped to show how he became Mrs. Baniszewski's attorney. Judge Rabb ruled that that would be irrelevant. On further objection by lawyers for the child defendants that Hammond's testimony would violate their attorney–client privileges, Rabb stopped Hammond's testimony altogether.

His first two ploys meeting with a minimum of success, Erbecker then put his client, Gertrude Baniszewski, on the witness stand. It was 10:55 a.m. on Tuesday, May 10, 1966.

17

A "PASSIVE PERSONALITY"

GERTRUDE BANISZEWSKI appeared wan and sleepy as she began in a soft, weak voice to tell of the hardships of her 37 years. Her tale of woe was credible enough until she began to relate her knowledge of the murder of Sylvia Likens, and then it soon became obvious that she either was lying or had a notoriously poor memory. Later, an hour and 11 minutes of relentless cross-examination by Leroy New brought out numerous discrepancies in her testimony.

Gertrude testified that she at first refused to take in Sylvia and Jenny but bowed to their imploring father. She went on to say that she was sick in bed much of the time Sylvia lived with her, and that she never harmed Sylvia.

Gertrude choked back tears as she told of prior hardships. "It was a real run-down home," she said of the house at 3850 East New York Street, "but it was all I could afford at the time."

"I believe I tried paddling her once," she said of

Sylvia. But did she ever "strike, beat or kick" her in October? "No, sir, I did not!"

Her direct testimony continued at 1:34 p.m., after the noon recess. A bit chilly in the air-conditioned courtroom, she had slipped a brown cardigan over her sleeveless blue sweater.

Gertrude said she did not recall any events the last few days of Sylvia's life except a couple of trips to the doctor. "I remember handing them a note," she added, about the note she gave to policemen. "I don't know which one of the children gave it to me." Other than fights, she had seen no mistreatment of Sylvia by the children, either. "Sometimes I would try to break it up," she said of the fighting; but generally, she said, she was too weak or sick to break it up.

On cross-examination, New confronted her with numerous contradictions between her trial testimony and the testimony she had given before the Marion County grand jury.

Although she told the trial jury she did not recall being out of bed on October 26, the day Sylvia died, and had not been upstairs or in the basement (her bedroom was on the first floor), her grand jury testimony had been that the "smell in the basement . . . was gagging me, and I started, you know, wanting to vomit, so I came back up," and, "When I went upstairs that one time, her eyes were open then." New asked her if she recalled that grand jury testimony. "I really don't remember what I did at the time," she replied, showing signs of belligerence.

"In any event," New said, "you were not sleeping."

She told the trial jury she did not recall saying anything to Sylvia as the girl lay incoherent in the basement on October 26. But her grand jury testimony had been, "I asked her to please come up and let them clean her up."

"Why did you want her upstairs instead of downstairs?" asked the deputy prosecutor.

"Were you lying to the grand jury?" he asked. "Are you lying to *this* jury?"

She replied, "No, sir!" to both questions.

New, who had been energetically pacing the floor between the prosecutor's table and the witness stand, arching his eyebrows and breathing like a dragon exhaling flame, drew out the horrid autopsy photographs of Sylvia's fantastically mutilated nude body. "I have seen that," she snapped, "and if you don't mind, I don't want to see it again."

But New shoved the photos under her nose, and she recoiled, her mouth gaping.

"Why don't you want to look at this girl's body?" he asked.

"I don't think anything dead is very pleasant to look at," she said.

"Now, did Sylvia have sores on her body?" New asked.

"No—not to my knowledge," the woman said.

"Now, the fact is," New said, "you're lying, aren't you?"

"No, sir," she said.

"Now, as a matter of fact," New said, "you beat

this little girl and scalded her with hot water, Mrs. Baniszewski?"

"No, sir, I did not," she said. She said she was not blaming the children for injuring Sylvia, either. New asked her whether testimony and signed statements of others, including her own children, contained lies. She said yes. Asked why her son Johnny would lie about her, she said, "I imagine he's a pretty scared little boy."

"Are *you* scared?" New asked.

"I've been scared about a lot of things for a long time," she said.

"Did Reverend Julian lie to this jury?" New asked.

"He most certainly did!" she said.

"I think that's all," said New, concluding his cross-examination. Gertrude was cross-examined briefly by the other defense lawyers, and then Erbecker tried to recoup some of his losses with additional questions. But soon Mrs. Baniszewski began to twist in the witness chair, complaining, "My back is hurting pretty bad." Court was adjourned early, at 4:16 p.m.

When court reconvened at 9 a.m. the next day, Wednesday, May 11, Deputy Prosecutor New had a few omitted questions to ask. To counterattack Erbecker's suggestion that Mrs. Baniszewski went before the grand jury on poor advice from her previous lawyer, John Hammond, New introduced in evidence the waiver of immunity she had signed before testifying. It set out clearly that she did not have to testify and that any testimony she gave could be used against her.

Before the waiver was allowed into evidence, Erbecker gained permission for preliminary questioning to determine whether Mrs. Baniszewski knew what she was signing. "Did you know," he asked, "that what you were signing could conceivably send you to the electric chair?" New's objection was sustained.

New then brought out more grand jury testimony to conflict with her testimony the previous day, in which she said she had spent much of October in bed sick. She had told the grand jury, "I never got to go to bed. You see, I've got children . . ."

When Erbecker regained the witness, he began to ask more questions about John Hammond. Erbecker said he was attempting to show that Hammond dealt all the Baniszewski cases out to other attorneys after the grand jury investigation. Objection sustained. "Hammond's not on trial," Judge Rabb reminded.

Erbecker's next witness was young, crew-cut Dr. William A. Shuck Jr., Marion County jail physician. He confirmed that Gertrude was a chronic sufferer of asthma and bronchitis. He added that she had had a severe rash about the face and neck at the time of her arrest, probably eczema. He said he had prescribed a tranquilizer, Thorazine, for her.

On cross-examination, New asked Dr. Shuck whether he believed Gertrude to be sane or insane. "I have no opinion," the doctor said. But he said he saw nothing to indicate she was insane.

Sound asleep in a chair in the courtroom antechamber as Dr. Shuck testified was another man, about 40, dark-complexioned, neatly dressed. A newspaper photographer was having fun snapping pictures of him in his slumber. He was soon called as the next witness for Gertrude Baniszewski, and he identified himself as Jerome Joseph Relkin, a psychologist. His credentials were a bachelor's degree in psychology from Rutgers University in 1950, a master's from Temple University in 1959, practical completion of his course work for a Ph.D. in clinical psychology from Purdue University, and internships at the Dr. Norman M. Beatty Memorial State Mental Hospital in Westville, Indiana, and the Larue D. Carter Memorial State Mental Hospital in Indianapolis.

He was writing his dissertation in criminal psychology, specifically in the areas of "aggressive" and "impulsive" behavior. He had tested and interviewed Gertrude Baniszewski for three hours in the jail the previous Sunday. Tests he had given her included the Thematic Apperception Test and the "hand test," a relatively new test designed to find a subject's potential for overt aggressive behavior, he said. The "hand test," he said, had been worked out by a couple of psychiatrists about three years before, and he was doing research on it himself. It involved showing subjects a series of pictures of hands and gauging their reactions.

Relkin had shuffled to the stand and chosen to "affirm" rather than "swear" that his testimony would be the truth and nothing but the truth.

He testified that Gertrude, "rather than being sadistic, is masochistic; she has a need to be punished herself."

On the issue of legal sanity, Relkin was not much help to Erbecker. "She is not psychotic," he said. "She knows right from wrong."

But he did back up Gertrude's denial. "Her story is probably true," he said. "She just became overwhelmed with all those children.

"When the children started to take over, I really believe her that she really went on drugs—and withdrew. She would wake up, take more drugs, and go back to sleep. She was overwhelmed, psychologically. She just crumbled, and they all took over."

He said her personality was "very inconsistent" with that of someone who would harm people.

"Is she aggressive?" asked Erbecker.

"No, not at all," said the witness. And he said, "She has a great need to be loved."

Relkin was all but destroyed that afternoon in cross-examination by Leroy New and Forrest Bowman.

"No impulsive behavior pattern?" New asked.

"I would not consider it impulsive, no," the psychologist said.

New referred to Relkin's drawing evidence of masochism from the fact that Gertrude had been beaten by her mate. "Did she say she enjoyed that?" he asked.

"No," Relkin admitted, "she did not say that." But she had indulged in masochistic behavior "by allowing herself to be beaten by her lover" and "allowing her children to take over," he said.

"How would she react toward hostility toward her?" asked Bowman, attorney for Coy and Johnny.

"She would take it," the witness said.

"How would she react to a harsh examiner?" Bowman had in mind Leroy New's brutal cross-examination of Mrs. Baniszewski the day before, in which she became defiant and outspoken.

"She would probably break down and cry," said Relkin.

"Would she get sarcastic?"

"No."

"Do you have an opinion as to *your* type of personality?" Bowman asked the psychologist.

"Certainly I do."

"Let me say," the lawyer continued, searching for a phrase, "do you have passive or defensive traits . . . what's the danger?"

"Many times," Relkin answered, "a psychologist puts his own traits into the results."

"Would you describe Mrs. Baniszewski as a warm, loving, affectionate woman?" asked Bowman. Relkin said he would.

New had another question. "Would she be reluctant to call her daughter a liar?"

"Yes." In fact, Relkin said, he had told her that was what she would have to do to help herself.

"Did you encourage her to help herself?" asked New.

"Yes." No more questions.

Erbecker's next line of witnesses included four physicians and four jail matrons. The physicians, all of whom had treated Mrs. Baniszewski at one time or another, confirmed her long medical history of asthma, bronchitis, anxiety, a kidney infection, a nodule in the breast, indigestion, insomnia, tiredness, headaches, tension, and the eczema-like rash at the time of her arrest.

One of the doctors was Paul G. Lindenborg, who said he had treated Mrs. Baniszewski at his office on October 25, the day before Sylvia's death. Under cross-examination, he said he could find no record of having treated her on October 23, contradicting her testimony that she had gone to his office that morning.

The jail matrons testified that Gertrude looked very thin and sick at the time of her arrest, that she looked even worse than the haggard woman she was at this time. "She looks good to the way she was then," said Ella Mae Staples.

Jerome Relkin had provided the comic relief in the 2½-week-old courtroom drama. Erbecker's next witness, 11-year-old Marie Baniszewski, provided the pathos.

18

PERJURY

THE LITTLE girl in the baby blue dress, with rosy cheeks and curly blond hair, had been waiting in the antechamber about an hour, flanked by her elderly foster mother and her lawyer, John Hammond.

She entered the courtroom with those two adults, who took seats near the press table. She swore to tell the truth and wiped her eyes as she identified herself as Marie Baniszewski, 11 years old. Did she know why she was on the witness stand in Criminal Court, Division 2, Erbecker asked?

"I'm here to testify to see if my mama killed Sylvia Likens," she sobbed. So far as she could see, according to her testimony, her mama did not kill Sylvia Likens.

"Did you ever at any time see your mother strike her?"

"Only when she's bad."

She had once seen her mother paddle Sylvia, Marie said. Then she began sobbing again and stopped talking.

Erbecker had already scored. He moved for adjournment so that the girl could regain her composure overnight. "Let's go on," the judge said; "it's early yet." It was not quite 4:30 p.m.

Marie said she had never seen her mother hit Sylvia with a paddle or burn or scald her in all of September or October. Back near the press table, Marie's foster mother, a Mrs. Simpson, was fuming.

Marie said she saw the other children mistreat Sylvia, but her mother usually was sick in bed. "I was always by her side," she said. Often, she said, she was out of the house to get her mother a prescription. She said she walked to Dr. Lindenborg's office (which was more than four miles away through city traffic) "nine or six times" to get prescriptions.

Sylvia had never slept in the basement, Marie said. She said she had never heard her mother tell others to mistreat Sylvia, but she had heard her tell them not to. Food was never denied to Sylvia, she said.

Her mother had gone to the doctor's office "about 11 o'clock" on October 23, the day Sylvia was branded, Marie said. "11 a.m. or 11 p.m.?" Erbecker asked. "In the afternoon," Marie said.

"Did you ever see your mother hurt Sylvia in any way?" Erbecker asked her.

"No," she said. Erbecker had no more questions, and court was adjourned.

At the beginning of his questioning, Erbecker had established Marie's competence to testify by asking her whether she knew what happened to little girls

who lied. "They get punished," she said. She cried
as she spoke the words.

John Hammond was mad. He had not expected
Marie to be called as a defense witness by Erbecker,
and he had not known that Erbecker and Mrs. Baniszewski had had a private conversation with Marie
the day before. Just before she testified, she was called
into another conference with her mother and Erbecker
in a small room adjoining the court. Hammond accompanied Marie into the room but left after about a
minute. "I didn't like the conversation," he said. He
reported that Erbecker was asking Marie leading
questions such as, "You never did see your mother do
anything to anybody else, did you?" Erbecker did not
put words into the girl's mouth, Hammond said, but
he was essentially repeating the mother's testimony
and the girl was affirming it. Hammond said Marie
indicated she did not want him, her own lawyer, in
the room.

During Marie's testimony, Gertrude fixed her
eyes on the girl, nodding yes or no with almost every question. A deputy sheriff noticed it and reported it to a deputy prosecutor. There would be
more on the subject the next day.

As court convened, Erbecker complained that he
had been denied permission to talk to one of his witnesses. The witness was Marie Baniszewski, the de-
nier was John Hammond; and Hammond reported
to the court that he merely had advised Marie not to
have any more private conversations with her mother's lawyer.

Before Marie was cross-examined, a deputy sheriff was taken as a witness out of order. He was a medical assistant and merely confirmed some of Dr. Shuck's testimony.

Then Erbecker asked the judge for permission to consult with his witness. "We had some omitted questions," he explained.

Deputy Prosecutor New objected strenuously. "At this time," he said indignantly, "I would like to tell the court the State of Indiana got this witness on cross-examination last night," meaning that, as a point of order, the state now had the floor to ask the witness questions. "We have reason to believe," New continued, "this witness has been persuaded to lie on the stand. And it is objectionable if Mr. Erbecker would talk to her."

Rabb ruled it would be out of order to allow Erbecker to confer with Marie now, but he instructed John Hammond that Erbecker had a right to talk with Marie when the cross-examination was finished.

Suddenly, Gertrude slumped in her chair, complaining of shortness of breath. Erbecker asked for a recess. Rabb ordered that Dr. Shuck be summoned from General Hospital; the trial would go on until he arrived. The call for Dr. Shuck and a resuscitator sparked rumors through the City-County Building that Gertrude had suffered a heart attack.

Marie, wearing a yellow dress, appeared paler than yesterday.

New, who had debated during the night whether

to cross-examine Marie himself or have Marjorie Wessner attempt the job, began the questioning, gently.

Marie cried almost from the start.

"Now, Marie," New said soothingly, "can you tell me why you're crying?"

"I'm nervous," the girl said.

New ran over details of the crime with her, particularly the ones she said she had seen the other children commit. She said Johnny once hit Sylvia "as hard as he could."

"Was your mother there when this happened?" New asked.

"Yes, sir," Marie said.

New asked about the time Johnny tied Sylvia in the basement. "You do your best, Marie," he said. "If you were down there, I want you to tell everything you remember."

New handed Marie the fraternity paddle; and her foster mother, in the courtroom again this morning, clasped her hands to her face. Marie said her mother had applied it two or three times to Sylvia's bottom.

"Did she ever hit her anywhere else?" New asked.

"No, sir!" Marie said.

New summoned Darlene McGuire into the courtroom. Marie had testified the day before that Darlene, one of Sylvia's best friends, had put a cigarette out on Sylvia. Confronting Marie with Darlene staring her in the face, New asked her if she still remembered that. Marie stuck to her story.

She said the branding occurred on a Tuesday the week before Sylvia died. Richard Hobbs, Shirley and Johnny Baniszewski, and Mrs. Baniszewski were present, she said.

"Then there was no school that day?" New asked.

"No," Marie said, but she could not think what holiday it might be, on October 19.

Marie said she had just come up from the basement and saw Ricky scratching the letter "I" on Sylvia's stomach. Shirley had heated the needle with a match, Marie said.

"Now, Marie," New cautioned. "Shirley said you lit the match. Who is telling the truth?" Marie was telling the truth, Marie insisted. She also insisted that her mother was in bed and had nothing to do with the branding or tattooing.

"Now, Marie," New admonished, "you're not telling the truth, are you?"

"Yes, I'm telling the truth!" New confronted her with contradictory testimony. "No, sir," she admitted, sobbing.

Marie said Paula lit the paper in the sink to heat the makeshift branding iron. "Now, Marie," New reminded, "Shirley says you're the one who lit the paper, and you stood there and watched. Is Shirley not telling the truth, or are you not telling the truth?"

Marie reddened; tears welled in her eyes. She seemed about to burst. "O God help me!" she blurted, tears gushing.

"Do you think you can tell us, Marie, really what

happened?" New asked. Marie admitted heating the tattooing needle herself.

Richard Hobbs had been at school, she mentioned. "I thought you said there wasn't any school?" New reminded.

Sylvia was branded a different day—Monday—Marie explained.

"A school day?"

"Yes. It was after school."

"Then Richard Hobbs was not in school."

"I forgot what happened," Marie said.

"Did you talk to your mother and Mr. Erbecker yesterday before you testified?" New asked her.

"Yes, sir," she said. "We talked about if Mom did anything wrong." She said neither Erbecker nor her mother had told her to lie.

New returned to the subject of matches. "Did you ever see your mother burn Sylvia?"

"Yes, sir," she admitted, "with a match."

"Did you see her hit her with a belt?"

"Yes, sir." New brought out the belt. Marie said she herself had been beaten with the large, leather police belt when they lived in Beech Grove.

New asked where she had got the matches to heat the tattooing needle. "From Mom." She restated that Richard Hobbs was the only one who used the needle, from the beginning.

"Now, Marie," New resumed, "are you trying to protect your mother?"

She again burst into tears. "The truth has to be

told," she sobbed. But she insisted that Gertrude did not participate.

New confronted the child with Richard Hobbs' signed statement in which he admitted branding Sylvia. "You testified that Paula was the one who held the hot iron?"

"I guess I'm mistaken," Marie admitted. "Ricky Hobbs really done it."

Marie's testimony now was coming free and easy; there were no more tearful interruptions. New reminded her of her difficulty the day before. "Are you telling the truth today?" he asked.

"Yes, sir," she said. When asked about the basement bath of garden hose and detergent Sylvia received, Marie said, "Mom was in on it too."

Marie had testified that Sylvia was unclean. "Who told you that?" New demanded.

"I don't remember," she said, looking downward.

"When you said that yesterday, that wasn't true, was it?"

"No, sir."

She changed her story of walking to Dr. Lindenborg's office to say she had ridden a bicycle there.

New asked about the judo flips. He asked Marie to step down before the jury. Standing nearly twice as tall as the little girl, the deputy prosecutor held out his large, rough hand and asked Marie several times to grasp it as if she were going to flip him. She stood back and explained it in words but feared to touch him.

Was Gertrude ever present during the judo flips,

New asked? "Yes, sir," Marie replied. "She'd just sit there and crochet." She admitted hearing her mother say, during Sylvia's fight with Anna Siscoe, "Let them fight their own battles."

The scraping heard by Mrs. Vermillion, Marie testified, was Paula firing the furnace, at 1 a.m. "I know, because I always kissed Paula good-bye."

"Now, Marie, that didn't happen, did it?" New scolded.

"I heard them at 1 o'clock," she insisted. "Paula was getting ready to go to work."

"At 1 o'clock in the morning?"

"She always went to work early. Our clock didn't work too good." Paula was due at her cafeteria job at 8 a.m.

New eyed the clock in the rear of the courtroom now. He asked for the noon recess. Marie had undergone more than two hours of cross-examination by one of the toughest examiners in the state, and she was not through yet.

In about 20 minutes that afternoon, Marie also admitted to New that she had seen her mother whip Sylvia and hold her head under running, scalding water.

It was George Rice's turn to cross-examine. He knew that Marie attended Sunday school faithfully, and he asked her if she had read in the Ten Commandments, "Thou shalt not bear false witness against thy neighbor." Marie said yes, she knew that meant to tell the truth.

"Would you say you violated that commandment yesterday?" Rice asked her.

"I guess," she stated hesitantly, "I would have to say no. I was confused yesterday; I was sort of mixed up today."

She said she loved both her mother and Paula, Rice's client, and added that when Paula brought home her wages, "She handed half of it to Mom, and kept half of it to herself, and gave all us kids an allowance, too."

Attorney Forrest Bowman asked Marie again whether she had told the truth the previous day. "Yes and no," she said. But she said that everything she had said today was the truth.

"You haven't told any lies today?" Bowman insinuated.

"Yes, sir," Marie answered quickly. "Ooops!" she said, clapping her hand to her mouth, realizing her mistake. Nearly everyone in the courtroom, including Judge Rabb and Marie herself, laughed.

"Marie," Bowman said, "you like to agree with people when they ask you questions, don't you? . . . You like to get along with people, don't you?"

"Yes, sir," she said; and Bowman skillfully led her through a series of five more "Yes, sir" answers to prove his point.

Then Marie admitted that she knew that her mother had started the tattoo.

Bowman asked her how Erbecker made her feel. "He had me confused yesterday," she said.

"Did anybody tell you to tell the jury that Richard Hobbs, Coy Hubbard, Johnny and Paula did things your mother did?" Bowman asked.

"No, sir," she said.

"Did anybody *confuse* you so you might tell the jury something besides the truth?"

"Yes, sir," she said.

"*Who* got you confused?" asked lawyer James Nedeff, when his turn came.

"Mr. Erbecker," Marie said. "I didn't know what to say, and I was afraid I'd say something wrong."

"When you said, 'O God help me!'," Nedeff said, "that's when you decided to tell the truth?"

"Yes, sir."

Marie, Erbecker, Mrs. Baniszewski and John Hammond had another short talk in the conference room during the ensuing recess. When court resumed, Erbecker had a few questions for Marie.

During the talk they just had, "I did not say anything at all at any time, did I?"

"No, sir."

"Now, you're not confused now, are you?"

"No, sir."

"Yesterday, didn't I tell you to tell the truth no matter who it hurt?"

"Yes, sir."

"Isn't it a fact—" Erbecker began.

"Objection to the form of the question," interrupted Forrest Bowman. Sustained.

Erbecker may have saved his reputation with those few questions, but his 11-year-old witness had been thoroughly discredited.

19

THE DEFENDANTS REST

ERBECKER CALLED two more witnesses that Thursday after Marie left the stand, both hospital librarians prepared to introduce voluminous records pertaining to Gertrude's medical history. Each volume contained about 50 pages. Judge Rabb refused to allow their admission into evidence because they failed to qualify under technical rules laid down by the Indiana Supreme Court. It was just as well, perhaps. Contained in one of the volumes was a report in which a doctor quoted Gertrude as saying she was not sure she had the right lawyer. That could have been grounds for mistrial.

Mrs. Baniszewski's chief witness on Friday, May 13, was a taxi driver who said his records showed he took someone from 3850 New York Street to "3048 Arlington Avenue" on October 23, 1965. It tended to corroborate Mrs. Baniszewski's assertion that she went to Dr. Lindenborg's office, which was at 3016 North Arlington, that day. The cabbie,

Uyless Pack, testified on cross-examination that he was not sure Mrs. Baniszewski had been his passenger or whether he went to 3048 North Arlington or 3048 *South* Arlington, which would have placed them near Gertrude's old hometown of Beech Grove.

Other witnesses called by Erbecker included two insurance agents, an attorney, and a deputy county clerk. By the clerk, the attorney was trying to show that Gertrude's ex-husband was delinquent in child support, but the clerk's testimony was not admitted, for technical reasons. By the attorney, Erbecker was showing that Mrs. Baniszewski had filed suits against Dennis Wright for support. By the insurance agents, he showed that she was unable to afford to continue her insurance payments. Finally, at 2:10 p.m., Erbecker announced that he was ready to rest his case, with the exception of one minor witness to be called the next week.

At the beginning of the day, Forrest Bowman withdrew the insanity pleas of Coy Hubbard and Johnny Baniszewski. Bowman and Paula's attorney, George Rice, would rest their cases quickly. Their three clients declined to take the stand.

Rice's first witness for Paula was her father, John S. Baniszewski Sr., 39 years old, former suburban policeman and now a troubleshooter at an East Side RCA plant. Rice was trying to show discipline problems that might have arisen from Gertrude's handling of the children, but objections to most of his questions—on grounds that they were irrelevant to the issues at trial—were sustained.

In some instances, however, Rice was happy enough just for the jury to hear the questions, one of which was: "Do you recall that on October 27, 1964, at 8:30 p.m., before your then residence, Gertrude Baniszewski and Paula Baniszewski appeared there and Gertrude Baniszewski struck Paula Baniszewski forcibly two times, and over your objection said, 'I'll hit her any time, or way, or place I please!'?"

Another purpose Baniszewski served, so far as Richard Hobbs' attorney James Nedeff was concerned on cross-examination, was to testify that Dennis Wright was only 23 years old—thus supporting the theory that Gertrude was a siren for men and boys like Richard Hobbs.

Baniszewski was Paula's only witness. Forrest Bowman had the floor for brother Johnny.

The principal of Johnny's two witnesses was Helen Brand, recreation director of the Juvenile Center, who testified, "We have no difficulty controlling Johnny, no, sir." Bowman wanted to contradict Gertrude's testimony that Johnny was hard to control. Bowman's other witness for Johnny was Policewoman Harriet Sanders, who testified that she was released from subpoena after her partner, Sgt. Leo Gentry, testified about Johnny's confession. The implication was that the prosecution was afraid to subject her to cross-examination.

For Coy Hubbard, Bowman called one witness—Coy's employer, James Moore, manager of Laughner's East 10th Street Cafeteria. He said Coy was a good worker and worked regularly from 4:30 p.m. to 8:30 p.m.—including Monday, October 25.

"Do you know if he hit a girl by the name of Sylvia on this date?" Leroy New asked on cross-examination. Moore did not.

Another dramatic high point was reached in the trial late that Friday afternoon as Richard Hobbs took the witness stand in his own defense. There was a feeling among courthouse observers that at least one of the children would have to take the stand, to explain his behavior, so that the jury would have some hook on which to hang its sympathy. Hobbs, who had performed a disgusting indignity to Sylvia's body, but who had not indulged in prolonged brutality as the others had, may have been the least vulnerable. But he soon was to find himself nonetheless quite pained by Leroy New's cross-examination.

Hobbs took the stand at 3:34 p.m. and told the jury in his deep but boyish voice that he had met the Baniszewski family in late July and thereafter became a frequent visitor at their home. He told the jury how he had gone there "just to visit" on Saturday, October 23, and wound up etching the words "I'm a prostitute and proud of it!" on a girl's stomach. He told how he stopped in again on Tuesday, October 26, on the way home from school to say "Hi" and returned to the Baniszewskis' about 5:30 p.m., after he had changed his clothes, had supper and done his homework.

He told of Gertrude's panic, his rescue attempts, Sylvia's death and the arrival of police.

"Well, the policeman was chasing everybody out of the house that wasn't a member of the family," the boy testified. "I went home and watched the rest of Lloyd Thaxton." Lloyd Thaxton was a clownish television disc jockey who had a nightly show for teenagers.

"Did you ever strike Sylvia Likens with anything?" the boy's attorney asked him.

"No, sir," the boy replied. Nor had he knocked her downstairs, or tied her up, or flipped her, or burned her with anything but the makeshift branding iron, he said. He did admit the tattooing, the branding, and striking her four or five times in the process.

"Gertrude told me to do the things on her abdomen," he explained. "I don't know why I hit her." He said he did not tell his father of his involvement until the day after his arrest. "He didn't take too much notice himself," the boy said; "he was too worried about Mom."

Up to now, the lad had been addressed as "Ricky." From here on, as Deputy Prosecutor Leroy New took over on cross-examination, he would be addressed contemptuously as "Mr. Hobbs."

"Now, you stated, Mr. Hobbs," New began, "that Sylvia Likens never did anything to you: Is that correct?"

"Yes."

New then had him step down from the witness stand and indicate to the jury, in the picture of Sylvia's body, which marks he had inflicted on her. He said that about three-fourths of the bruises in the autopsy photo were already on Sylvia when he began his tattoo.

New was forceful, loud, insinuating. "So in other words, Mr. Hobbs, there were massive cuts and bruises on this body when you were branding her: Is that correct?"

"Yes, sir."

"Now, it was your idea, Mr. Hobbs, to brand and mutilate this girl, wasn't it?"

"I don't know. It may have been my idea."

"Now, Gertrude Baniszewski didn't make you do it, did she?"

"No, sir."

Hobbs had testified that Sylvia flinched while she was being branded. "Did you ask her if it hurt?" New wanted to know.

"No, sir."

"What you did is hit her four or five times with the back of your hand, isn't it?"

"Yes, sir."

"And she begged you not to do that, didn't she?"

"No, sir, because I'd remember something like that."

"Did you smell the flesh when you burned her?"

"No, sir, it wasn't that hot." (Just hot enough to leave a big, red "3.")

"As a matter of fact, you don't care, do you, Mr. Hobbs?"

"At this time I do."

"Nobody made you do that, did they?"

"No, sir."

"Now the fact is, Mr. Hobbs, you've remembered only what you want to this afternoon, haven't you?"

"I imagine— I don't know."

"You weren't remorseful at all, were you? You felt no sorrow or pity?"

"No, sir. Not at the time."

"You just wanted to be mean to her, didn't you?"

"I imagine."

Hobbs' grizzled father, who had taken time off from a downtown construction project where he was foreman, sat in the gallery, staring at the floor.

"Instead of giving her artificial respiration," New suggested, "you kept your weight on her so she couldn't breathe, didn't you? You were tromping on her!"

"No, sir," the boy denied. It was 5:09 p.m. and court was adjourned, but New resumed his grilling Monday morning.

Hobbs had denied being at the Baniszewski house on October 25, in his testimony, but his signed confession said he thought Sylvia would be gone Tuesday, the 26th, "because Gertrude told me she was to get rid of Sylvia the night before."

"Now the fact is," New said, "you were at 3850 East New York Street the night of Monday the 25th, weren't you? You planned to get rid of Sylvia Likens."

"It must have been the truth if I signed it," the boy conceded. "I don't remember it now."

"Were you some particular friend of Gertrude?" New asked.

"I was a friend of the kids, too."

"Did you ever have sexual relations with Gertrude Baniszewski?"

"No, sir!" It was about the only time Hobbs raised his voice.

He said also he had not seen Gertrude make Sylvia drink urine. "Did you tell a reporter, Mr. Bob Hoover, you did?" New asked.

"No, sir," the boy said. "I don't remember talking to any reporter." A few minutes later, Hoover, a newsman for radio station WIBC, appeared in the courtroom; and New stood him in front of Hobbs. The boy said he still did not recall. Later, during presentation of rebuttal evidence, Hoover testified that he talked to Hobbs a few days after the murder. There was no mention of the cup of urine in the interview, however.

New asked the Hobbs boy whether he became sick during the branding.

"Kind of," he said.

"Kind of sick where?"

"I can't describe it."

"Sick with yourself?"

"Yes, sir."

"But you didn't stop."

Although New's cross-examination showed several inconsistencies in the boy's testimony, it would be hard to conclude that he lied deliberately. However, the cross-examination had been effective in making a case for premeditation and malice.

Nedeff's next witness for Hobbs was George Martin, the ex-cop who lived across the street. Following him was Barbara Jean Hobbs, 18 years old, the boy's pretty, brown-haired sister. Both were character witnesses. Except for the boy's minister, to be called as another character witness later in the afternoon, Nedeff rested his case. The minister, the Rev. Willard J. Doyle of the Grace Methodist Church, said, "I have no better family in the church" than the Hobbs family. "Their home is a Christian home."

It was time for the state's rebuttal evidence.

Bob Hoover was the first witness. The second was Joseph Relkin, the psychologist who had testified earlier for Mrs. Baniszewski.

Sportily attired in a plaid coat with a carnation in the lapel, he again walked to the stand and affirmed to tell the truth. New recalled his testimony that he had served an internship at Larue D. Carter Memorial State Mental Hospital. "Did you neglect to tell the jury," New asked, "that you were also a *patient* there in the psychiatric ward?"

"He didn't ask me that," the embarrassed psychologist said. But he admitted it was true. As a matter of fact, Relkin and the lawyer who called him, Erbecker, had been patients at Larue Carter at the same time. But Erbecker swore he met Relkin after his release from the hospital.

Other rebuttal witnesses included Anna Siscoe,

Darlene McGuire, and Stephanie Baniszewski, who was still charged with murder. The Siscoe girl said that she had had only the one fight with Sylvia, after Gertrude had told her that Sylvia had impugned her character.

Darlene McGuire denied putting a cigarette out on Sylvia.

Stephanie Baniszewski was on the witness stand a good part of the day and proved to be almost as interesting a witness as Relkin, Marie Baniszewski, or Randy Lepper. She would toss her long hair about and reflect on each question with the eye of a lawyer, which is what she said she wanted to be.

She testified, among other things, that Richard Hobbs had dropped Sylvia's head on the stair steps as they carried her upstairs on October 26. Hobbs had denied it. Stephanie's testimony indicated that that could have been an accident, however. Stephanie's testimony raised a few other contradictions in Ricky's testimony, and she added a few details and confirmed some others in the already established state's case.

On cross-examination, Erbecker sought to expose the "deal" he said the state had made with Stephanie. She testified that she had talked with her mother in the jail lunchroom about the possibility of becoming a state's witness. "I told my mother that if I thought I should, I would," she said. "She said I must not love her." Stephanie began crying then, and added, "I'm just here in the hope I can help anybody."

"Including yourself?" Erbecker sneered.

"I don't care what happens to me," she said.

Erbecker asked about the "deal."

"Sir," Stephanie replied, "if they had made a deal, I would have refused it."

She testified that Gertrude was hysterical at many times.

"What does hysterical mean?" Erbecker asked.

"Hysterical means calm," said Stephanie.

Unlike Marie, Stephanie refused to be led by Erbecker's questions. When he asked, "As a matter of fact, everybody around the house was accusing Sylvia of doing something, isn't that right?" she answered, "No, sir."

"You know what it means to turn state's evidence, don't you?" Erbecker asked her.

"Yes," she said, "it means to go over to the other side."

"And you're here to help everybody but yourself, aren't you?" Erbecker asked sarcastically.

Stephanie sobbed. "They probably think I came in here because I want to hang everybody too, but I don't," she cried.

Stephanie said she could describe her feelings for her mother and her sister Paula "in three words." What were those words, asked Paula's attorney, George Rice? "I love her." But her mother "doesn't believe it," she added.

Stephanie loved her boyfriend, Coy Hubbard, too; and, interestingly, her testimony did not recall any brutality on his part. How long had he been her boyfriend, New asked?

"He said always," sighed Stephanie.

Except for one last, ludicrous appearance on the witness stand by Gertrude, that was the end of adversary evidence. But for psychiatrists' testimony and final argument, the case was ready for the jury.

20

NEUROTIC BUT NOT PSYCHOTIC

GERTRUDE BANISZEWSKI had her handkerchief to her face; she was weeping and complaining of severe shortness of breath. It was shortly after 9 a.m. on Tuesday, May 17, 1966, in the fifth week of her trial for murder. She insisted on going back to the witness stand in rebuttal; her attorney, William Erbecker, said it was against his advice. She barely gasped out her testimony. Was it just another attack of asthma, or was she finally realizing the gravity of her situation? Her testimony varied little from her earlier testimony and added little.

Three court-appointed psychiatrists followed Gertrude to the stand and testified, one after the other, that they believed the woman was sane now and was at the time of the crime. All other defendants had withdrawn their insanity pleas. The doctors stuck to their opinion through a total of more than two hours of prodding cross-examination by Erbecker.

"I don't believe that she's ever been psychotic,"

said Dr. Dwight W. Schuster. "She had what is commonly termed nervousness."

Schuster added on cross-examination that she might even be psychoneurotic, or neurotic, but not out of touch with reality. After about 10 minutes, Gertrude pleaded to the bailiff for help. Court was recessed, and Gertrude was given first aid for her "attack."

When court reconvened, Erbecker asked the doctor what he thought of the savage torture inflicted on Sylvia. "This does not necessarily mean," Dr. Schuster said, "that this was sadism. I think these things can occur with a person who is in contact with reality.

"I have not said she does not have some emotional problems," he added. "I think she knew what she was doing and could have controlled herself."

"Would you recommend this defendant, Gertrude Baniszewski, for a baby-sitter job?" her attorney asked. Objection sustained.

Dr. Schuster added in response to questions by Leroy New that Gertrude had been vague with him when he interviewed her. He said she told him, "I don't know the whole story; Mr. Erbecker doesn't want me to say."

Dr. Dewitt W. Brown was next. He said he did not use the terms "sane" and "insane"; but he said, "In my opinion, she was not psychotic or mentally ill at that time."

He said she had some impaired memory, however, possibly through use of "the mental mechanism of denial, a trick that we all use to control or repress things in the unconscious."

On cross-examination, Dr. Brown came to the aid of the discredited psychologist, Relkin. "Most of her life," he said of Mrs. Baniszewski, "she's been a relatively passive person; she's been able to keep most of her hostilities repressed." But such repression, he said, can be broken with temper outbursts.

Dr. Brown finished at 12:42 p.m. Judge Rabb had declined to call a lunch recess at noon. Somewhat tested by Erbecker's lengthy but futile cross-examination, he said he did not want to keep the doctors waiting. However, Gertrude complained of sickness again, and the judge did grant a five-minute recess. Dr. Ronald H. Hull took the stand at 12:52 p.m. He said he had not found any indication that Gertrude ever was insane. As for her vagueness in relating events leading to Sylvia's death, he said, "I felt she was feigning it."

"Did you testify previously, in a habeas corpus hearing, that she had a tendency to paranoid thinking?" asked Erbecker.

"No," the psychiatrist said. Erbecker confronted him with the habeas corpus transcript, quoting him as saying, "She had some tendencies toward paranoid thinking, but not paranoid delusions."

"Yes, I was wrong," the doctor admitted. But he added, "Paranoid thinking is a very common thing." Erbecker launched into a long series of questions, detailing the horror of the crime, asking the doctor with each detail whether it would change his opinion of Gertrude's sanity. The lawyer then launched into a long series of questions about sadism and neurosis.

Deputy Prosecutor New had let Erbecker question the first two doctors freely, but now he had had enough. He began objecting to each question as irrelevant and repetitious. Judge Rabb sustained objections to eight consecutive questions by Erbecker. "Am I precluded from cross-examining this witness?" Erbecker asked.

"You are not precluded," Rabb replied. "Make it cross-examination, please." At this juncture, New asked to be heard with the jury out of the courtroom. The jury was ushered out, and New stated, "We think this has reached the point of abuse. Mr. Erbecker is trying to incite and try the patience of everybody in this courtroom. He has the responsibility to behave himself in the courtroom in a first degree murder trial, and we are going to ask that he be censured."

Forrest Bowman, defense attorney for Coy Hubbard and Johnny Baniszewski, had something to say. Although he did not wholly agree with Mr. New, he said, he did say that he was getting hungry and the jury probably was too, and the jury could not therefore hear evidence with any degree of clarity. It was 1:36 p.m. Rabb reluctantly granted a recess for lunch. He did not rule on New's motion to censure Erbecker.

After lunch, Erbecker completed his cross-examination in 13 minutes. A defense-employed psychiatrist also had examined Gertrude, but Erbecker did not even bother to put him on the stand. There was no direct testimony that Gertrude was insane; yet the next day Erbecker threw all his cards into the insanity plea.

After an unsuccessful attempt by Erbecker to introduce the transcript of the habeas corpus hearing, the attorneys settled down to discussing instructions to the jury. Erbecker tendered 193 of his own suggested instructions, and Rice and Bowman tendered nearly 50 apiece. New tendered none, and Nedeff tendered none. Some of Erbecker's would have instructed the jury that the state "has failed to discharge the burden of proof in this case."

Rabb already had 62 of the court's own instructions to read to the jury; and he said he would decide overnight which, if any, of the defendants' instructions to accept. Attorneys combed through the proposed instructions for two hours late that Thursday afternoon. They bantered and joked with each other, but others in the courtroom were tense. Mrs. Baniszewski sat silent. Mr. and Mrs. Ralph Hubbard, Coy's parents, waited in the gallery after other spectators had left, to get a word with their son when court adjourned at 5:30 p.m. Ricky Hobbs lit a cigarette before being led away by a deputy sheriff.

The next morning, Judge Rabb announced that he had accepted 11 instructions tendered by Erbecker, three by Bowman, and two by Rice.

The instructions included Indiana's legal definition of murder: "Whosoever purposely and with premeditated malice kills any human being is guilty of murder. . . ."

They included also one applicable to Johnny Baniszewski, who was 12 years old when Sylvia died, and to Richard Hobbs, who was 14 at the time: "An infant between the ages of 7 and 14 is presumed to be incapable of committing crimes, but the presumption may be rebutted by proof that the infant possessed sufficient discretion to be aware of the nature of the act."

And this instruction on sanity: "When there is mental capacity sufficient to fully comprehend the nature and consequences of an act, and unimpaired will power strong enough to master an impulse to commit a crime, you may find there is criminal responsibility."

21

"THE PENALTY SHOULD BE DEATH"

DEPUTY PROSECUTOR Marjorie Wessner, who had been silent through most of the trial, rose to deliver the state's summation. She described the testimony as "horrible, stomach-wrenching," the accounts of "a beastly, beastly crime."

She again showed the jury the smiling portrait of Sylvia Likens. "She seems to be looking forward to the future," Miss Wessner said, "to future joys and happy experiences. . . .

"Sylvia, being the obedient girl she was, tried to please Mrs. Baniszewski and said nothing of the mistreatment. . . .

"The series of brutally outrageous acts on these girls equals only the horrible torture of prisoners in German war camps."

Richard Hobbs' head drooped toward his lap as it had through most of the trial. The other defendants sat erect and expressionless. Paula attempted to whisper something to her attorney but was shushed.

Miss Wessner, stumbling occasionally over the

name Baniszewski, continued. She picked up the paddle and the belt, saying, "My head jarred when I heard the testimony that Sylvia was hit in the head with this board. My flesh could feel the sting of the metal on this belt. . . .

"Mrs. Baniszewski knew on Sunday she was going to hold these notes until she and the rest of the defendants had completed the murder of Sylvia."

Miss Wessner's voice broke as she related, "Sylvia said she felt like her teeth were coming out as she ate that rotten pear. . . .

"There was practically no fat on that girl's body. She hadn't eaten for a week! . . . We'll never know the pain and the suffering that Sylvia endured. The best evidence of that was the picture of her lips—lips that were bitten in shreds. . . .

"I wish she were here today, with eyes as in this picture, full of hope and anticipation."

William Erbecker made the first defense closing argument and shocked almost everyone from the start with his incredible speech. "Participating in this case was not of my choice," he said. "I was asked to. . . . This crime was horrible, horrendous, vicious. . . . I've been in a lot of murder trials, and this is the most vicious I ever saw in my life! It threatens the roots of civilization. . . .

"But we also see here an insane woman deprived of her constitutional rights. . . . And if I make some mistakes, please don't hold it against that poor, unfortunate woman." He said her going before the grand jury was "like sticking your head in a lion's den. As for Leroy New, I don't suppose he asked any illegal questions in there. He's a high-grade gentleman. He probably just went as far as the law would allow."

Erbecker paced up and down before the jury and began to raise his voice. His client, Gertrude Baniszewski, raised her hand to her mouth.

"In my opinion," the woman's own lawyer shouted, "she ought to go to the electric chair!"

When the shock abated, he added: "—if you think this is the action of a sane, normal person."

He picked up an autopsy photograph. "How can anybody look at that picture there," he said, "and say that she is sane?

"There is no motive in this case. That poor little girl, I feel sorry for her parents. That little girl had a right to live, to grow up, to get married and have children. And for anybody to tell you that that lady doesn't have a diseased mind. . . .

"Now the State of Indiana will ask for its revenge here. What will the electric chair do to this woman?" The lawyer launched into a gruesome description of an electrocution he had witnessed as a young man.

"I condemn her for being a murderess, that's what I do; but I say she's not responsible because she's not all here!"

Erbecker sometimes whispered, sometimes shouted; he wheedled and cajoled. "Look at this exhibit!" he commanded softly and incredulously, holding a photograph. "Look at the lips on that girl!"

The lawyer picked up the torture tools and laid

them on the table. "How sadistic can a person get?" he asked. "The woman is stark mad!" Paula began crying.

"I've done my little job," Erbecker concluded, saying that the psychiatrists had raised a reasonable doubt as to Gertrude's sanity. "If this woman is sane," he said, "put her in that chair. She committed acts of degradation that you wouldn't commit on a dog. Send her to the chair!"

But he modified the challenge: "She has to be crazy or she wouldn't have permitted that."

It was time for lunch.

Scholarly George Rice delivered the first argument of the afternoon, for Paula Baniszewski, promising to be "clear, logical and honest."

He decried the state's access to grand jury testimony and the fact that the defendants were being tried jointly. "The defendants are grouped together like a single target for the prosecutor to aim at. Though we sit at the same table, we are adverse to each other."

Rice listed what he considered all the evidence against Paula that could be gleaned from the testimony, and he said it did not add up to murder. But he did not mention the black eyes, the hitting of Sylvia's teeth with the cast, and the testimony that Paula had made a game of hitting Sylvia with whatever object was at hand. He minimized Paula's choking of Sylvia, "who, upon being released, walked away!"

He noted Paula's amazement when she was told that Sylvia had died. "Does a murderer express surprise?" He noted the 100-odd cigarette burns in

Sylvia's flesh. "Keep in mind that Paula Banisze-wski was a non-smoker."

Rice said he was at a loss to explain Sylvia's fail-ure to escape; but he said, "I do have something to say on the issue of motivation.

"We have dealt here with a family that has known chill penury for a long time. There was never suffi-cient money in the cookie jar. Consciously or uncon-sciously, there built up a feeling of anger against the world. There was no channel for its release until Sylvia Likens came to the household and provided a focal point."

Rice ended with a plea for the jury to consider the awful imprint a guilty verdict would have on Paula's "psyche. . . . She has gone through the indignity of being a young girl tried for murder in open court."

Forrest Bowman's closing argument, for Coy Hub-bard and Johnny Baniszewski, was barely audible. He sat on the corner of the defense table and practi-cally whispered to the jury, in a conversational tone.

"I would like about an hour," he said, "to tell you why a 15-year-old boy and a 13-year-old boy should not be put to death."

He wondered whether the murder had been the result of unconscious hostility and whether the in-dictment of children had been the result of more unconscious hostility on the part of the public.

He took a swing at Leroy New. "I don't like cross-examining children. But . . . the purpose is to ferret out the truth. It is not to ridicule, embarrass, abuse. . . .

"Shirley Baniszewski, 10 years old, was somehow prompted or persuaded to get on the witness stand. She may not realize the impact of that today. But someday, when she's 15 or 16, she's going to realize. . . .

"Johnny Baniszewski was too loyal to his family to get on the witness stand."

The young lawyer tried another side track. "Just how vigorous have our public officials been in preventing this kind of tragedy? Shocking as it is, it's not too surprising. It's just an accident that Sylvia Likens isn't on trial today—and Johnny Baniszewski dead. She just happened to be the target for all the frustration and hate."

Bowman criticized police tactics in questioning the youngsters. "Was the atmosphere like last Friday afternoon when Mr. New was cross-examining Richard Hobbs? . . .

"Johnny and Coy have some things in common," Bowman complained. "They can't make a contract or a will; they can't drive a car. They can't even buy a car without their parents' signature; they can't get married or purchase real estate, and, except for a major crime, they can't be tried in Criminal Court."

Even if convicted of the lesser, included offense of manslaughter, Johnny would have to serve two years at the State Reformatory, and Bowman predicted the harmful effect of that. "You might as well send him up there for life. . . .

"Now," Bowman asked, "who killed Sylvia Likens? We still don't know, for sure. . . .

"It appears to me that sometime Sunday, or Monday, somebody went on a rampage. I don't know who, but who had the capacity for violent behavior?" he asked, glancing toward Gertrude.

"Johnny, like Coy, is probably guilty of assault and battery," Bowman conceded, "but he's not charged with that, is he?"

He deplored the traumatic effect of the trial and possible conviction on each boy. "His life will never be the same."

James Nedeff, attorney for Richard Hobbs, began with regret. "Sylvia Likens," he said, "God bless her tortured and tormented soul. She did have a right to live. I in my own heart can't remember a girl so much sinned against and abused."

But he said blame for some abuse must be laid on her own family. He cited her parents and Jenny, "a sister who could limp three and a half miles to a park but couldn't walk two or three steps out into New York Street to beg for help."

Nedeff praised his client, Ricky Hobbs, for testifying. "There may be little variations and inconsistencies in his testimony, but he told the truth.

"I advised him, 'You'd be like a sparrow against an 88 howitzer cannon.' He said, 'He can't hurt me if I tell the truth.' So he was plunked from the witness stand by one of the greatest cross-examiners in this state, for the most savage and relentless cross-examination."

Nedeff stressed Ricky's short-term participation in the torture, saying, "If he hadn't put the words on her stomach, he would have been a state's witness, probably, rather than Stephanie."

The lawyer suggested that Gertrude drew Ricky into the mess. "Is that what attracted Ricky there? A woman who had two paternity suits filed against a man of 19 or 20, who danced to the music of a record player, a Lucrezia Borgia, a Lady Macbeth? That is for you to decide.

"Ricky Hobbs is guilty of a lot of things, but not guilty of murder. He is guilty of being a young man, a lad, of being under the influence of an older person, of being a follower and not a leader. I think he listened to the siren's song.

"Ricky Hobbs has paid and will continue to pay. Don't do Leroy New's dirty work for him."

Leroy New had one more job to do—to get the jury's minds off the defense lawyers' sentiments and back onto the issues at trial, in his closing argument in rebuttal.

"The prosecutors' job," he began, "is to present the evidence to the best of our ability." He said he would try to speak "through the mangled and shredded lips of Sylvia Likens. I see her wherever I look.

"There's no self-defense here, no provocation, no justification." Already New's voice, with its great range of inflection, sounded indignant. His long, lean body swayed to and from the jury with each inflection, hypnotically, like a palm tree in the breeze.

"It was planned, calculated, systematic, cold-blooded murder," he declared.

Answering Forrest Bowman's criticism of his putting children on the witness stand, he said, "Now, let's look at some of the responsibilities here. Each one of these five defendants had first and foremost the responsibility to leave Sylvia Likens alone. *We* had the responsibility to bring all the evidence we could find that could explain this crime." Answering the charge that he was brutal in cross-examination, he admitted, "We did bring up the heavy artillery. Now *your* duty," he said to the jury, "is the most solemn and most sickening. . . .

"The issue here," New insisted, "is not the electric chair or a hospital, but law and order. Will we allow such acts? Will we allow such brutality on a human being? . . .

"Where is the compassion, Mr. Nedeff?" The deputy prosecutor was whining indignantly. "I can't help but speak for Sylvia Likens. Not for the Hobbs boy, but for Sylvia Likens.

"Will we shy away from the most diabolical case ever to come before a court or jury? There isn't a shred of evidence in the testimony that Gertrude was ever insane.

"The time is here now," he said. Tension gripped the courtroom. You could tell something special was coming. Quoting from the scripture, New continued:

" 'When a man smiteth another man so that he dies, he also must be put to death!'

"If you go below the death penalty in this case,

you will lower the value of human life by that much for each defendant.

"Are we going to allow them to plead simply that their mother is dying of cancer? . . . because he's a 12-year-old, he's entitled to mercy?

"The blood of this girl will forevermore be on their souls—not on mine, and not on yours as jurors." New accused defense lawyers of trying to "hoodwink" the jury by shifting blame. He criticized their "brazen attitude" in rapping the prosecution for failing to identify the fatal blow.

"Every mark on that girl's body," New contended, "contributed directly to her death, and that was the testimony. The subdural hematoma was the ultimate blow.

"This is the most hideous thing Indiana has ever seen and I hope will ever see.

"I can't hear a word these people are saying," he cried, gesturing toward the defense lawyers, "because the voice of Sylvia Likens cries out to both God and man."

He recounted the callousness of the crime, then stated:

"The state makes no demand for anything. But it is my considered opinion that this has been the most terrible crime ever committed in the State of Indiana and deserves the most terrible penalty possible under the law of the State of Indiana.

"What you do here will have a profound effect on the behavior of children for the next generation. . . .

"All we hear is this whining appeal," he said of the defense's tear-jerking arguments, "anything but the blame where the blame belongs."

New felt obligated to explain Sylvia's failure to escape, however. "I think she trusted in man," he said. "I think she did not believe these people would do this to her and continue to do it. How can these defense counsel come in and ask that question, 'Why didn't she leave?' . . .

"Poverty has nothing to do with bestiality. I've lived in poverty myself."

New was finishing. "I don't envy you," he told the jurors. "It took courage, it took a great deal of patience for you to sit through this testimony.

"I say the verdict should be first-degree murder, and the penalty should be death."

New's argument, no doubt one of the greatest orations in American courtroom history, had taken only 34 minutes. Judge Rabb immediately launched into instructions, which took another half-hour. The jury began deliberation shortly after 5 p.m.

Supper was ordered for the jury in its deliberation room at the rear of the court. The courtroom emptied briefly as lawyers, newsmen and spectators went out for supper. They began drifting back in an hour.

George Rice and Leroy New discussed philosophy in Judge Rabb's chambers. Forrest Bowman and his pretty, pregnant wife, who had been a spectator throughout the trial, played euchre with newsmen in the antechambers; soon Bowman dropped out and

John Baniszewski Sr. joined the game. William Erbecker had gone home and gone to bed.

An untold number of cigars and cigarettes were smoked. Some observers were beginning to wonder whether the jury might "hang"—fail to reach a verdict. But the gallery was still half full of spectators at midnight.

Finally, about 1:30 a.m., the jury notified the bailiff it had a verdict. Newsmen rushed to telephones. Lawyers began to pace back and forth. Erbecker had been summoned from his home about an hour before to discuss the possibility of sending the jury to a hotel for the night.

The defendants, who had been kept in the jail during deliberation, tripped lightly into the courtroom at 1:40 a.m. Sheriff's deputies and policemen ringed the courtroom scene. The jury foreman handed the verdict forms to a bailiff, who handed them to the judge, who read the verdicts without hesitation.

Gertrude Baniszewski was guilty of first-degree murder and should be imprisoned for life in the Indiana Women's Prison.

Paula Baniszewski was guilty of second-degree murder and should be imprisoned for life in the Indiana Women's Prison.

Richard Hobbs, Coy Hubbard and Johnny Baniszewski all were guilty of manslaughter and should be imprisoned for two to twenty-one years in the Indiana State Reformatory. (Johnny would be the youngest inmate in the institution's history.)

Gertrude moaned as the verdicts were read. The

other defendants sat expressionless and colorless, then a few cried. They were sentenced, according to the jury's recommendations, the following Tuesday, May 24, 1966.

Many courthouse observers found the verdict satisfactorily selective, confirming the idea of a joint trial. But there were dissatisfied elements in the public. A woman called the court to ask, "What kind of crime do you have to commit in Indiana to get the electric chair?" The jurors had been ready to put Gertrude in the chair at one point in their deliberation, according to one report; but they came down to the life sentence to reach agreement on another part of the verdict.

Another woman wrote to a newspaper, "I did not agree with the jury. . . . Why should they [the defendants] be confined at our expense to live when they had no mercy whatsoever on that poor girl?"

A man wrote to the same newspaper: "Well, Indiana has done it again. . . . It's the only state in the union where you can get away with murder."

However, the electric chair was a somewhat less than real possibility. The state's governor had declared a moratorium on executions until the state legislature had time to consider a repeal of capital punishment, which was considered likely to pass.

The defendants went to prison, but their lawyers were filing appeals and motions to set aside the verdict. Many observers thought Gertrude Baniszewski was lucky to get away with her life. When Erbecker filed a motion for a new trial for her, one wag suggested that the meanest thing Judge Rabb could do would be to grant it.

The grand jury reconsidered the evidence against Stephanie Baniszewski and set her free, as expected. She went to live with her father. Her younger sisters and brothers remained in foster homes.

Paula Baniszewski found life in prison comfortable. It was the nicest bed she had ever had, she told her attorney.

Epilogue

IN HIS fifth-floor office in the City-County Building, overlooking the City Market, Leroy K. New was musing over events of the past five weeks. The conversation was casual; the men were in shirt sleeves. But New sounded earnest as he spoke of Jenny Likens, the innocent but guilt-ridden girl who had won her way into the hearts of prosecutor's deputies, police, newsmen, and other spectators.

"You know," New said, "somebody ought to do something for that girl." He leaned back in his chair, his hands folded behind his head, his eyes slightly elevated. "She ought to be in school. Her folks have a job lined up for her to answer the telephone for a taxicab company in Lebanon, but she'll be doing that when she's 50. She needs a new brace, too. . . ."

Within a few days, Leroy New did something for Jenny Likens. He virtually adopted her. With the help of others on the prosecutor's staff, he bought her a new brace. He enrolled her in North Central

High School, where he would take her every morning on his way to work from his home in suburban Carmel.

Jenny's parents had separated again but were talking of a reconciliation that might include rejoining the carnival. Either way, the prospect of further schooling had seemed dim for their 16-year-old daughter until the deputy prosecutor and his family invited her to come live with them. And Lester and Betty Likens could see the move as a wonderful opportunity for their daughter.

Jenny had been less than eager to return to school until New talked to her and she met his two well-bred daughters and began to share their enthusiasm. Soon they were sharing their time and their clothing with Jenny. How long Jenny would stay at the New home was indefinite. She might take some vocational training later, get a part-time job and rent a room of her own in the city. The important thing now was to get her back into a school-going atmosphere.

Before long, Jenny had her books; and, even before school began, she was working problems in mathematics, dividing fractions and such, and getting half the problems right, too. Her speech was still crude, but she was not dull. A brightness lurked deep in her dark, sad eyes.

Life was like a dream for Jenny Likens. She was learning to cook; she was learning to speak correctly; she was driving the tractor-lawnmower around New's huge yard; she was swimming every day in the neighbors' private pool. She loved her own parents, but Mr. and Mrs. New also had understandably worked their way into a warm spot in her heart. "I just wish," she told me, "me and Sylvia could have been left with people like this, instead of with Gertrude."

But because of Sylvia, Jenny's heart also bore a burden of guilt that would probably never dissolve entirely. Despite her rationalization of her failure to aid her dying sister, she would forever feel the weight of that failure. She would feel it especially heavy whenever she entered a church, without the sister who always had accompanied her to the altar.

Jenny Likens was fortunate, however. She had her life, she had love, she had a future. Others were not so lucky.

Danny and Benny Likens were at that very time roaming the dingy streets of Indianapolis' Near West Side. They had part-time jobs at a drive-in restaurant, but they were not making enough money to live on. A good part of what 19-year-old Danny was making, he was losing at a nearby pool hall. Sixteen-year-old Benny, Jenny's twin brother, was losing his ambition. In their financial trouble, the boys had been evicted from one boarding house and spent their nights wherever they could find shelter; sometimes it was just a doorway.

Where were Danny and Benny Likens headed? Like Jenny, they were not dull. They were likable. But was their fate to be vaguely equal to that which had befallen their late sister, Sylvia? If not so physically agonizing, at least excruciating in terms of the length of the misguided lives they might lead?

If a lesson was learned from the case of Sylvia Likens, now was the time to apply it. Were innocent children to suffer again from lack of concern and attention?

"The voice of Sylvia Likens cried out to God and man."

Afterword

THE CONVICTIONS of Gertrude and Paula Baniszewski were reversed on appeal by the Indiana Supreme Court, ruling 4 to 0 (with one abstention, by a justice who had worked for the Marion County Prosecutor) that the jury had been unduly prejudiced by pre-trial publicity and that separate trials should have been granted to the defendants. Gertrude was convicted of first-degree murder again in her second trial, in 1971 in Peru, Indiana, on change of venue, and again sentenced to life in prison. She was released on parole in 1985, on a 3–2 vote by the parole board. Paula, rather than face retrial, pleaded guilty to voluntary manslaughter in 1971, for a 2-to-21-year sentence, and served 2 more years in prison (she escaped twice, both before and after the reversal of her first conviction, but was recaptured each time).

Coy Hubbard, Ricky Hobbs and Johnny Baniszewski were released on parole in 1968.

Ricky Hobbs died in 1972, at the age of 21, of cancer.

Coy Hubbard was sent to prison again, for armed robbery, in 1978. And he was tried in 1983 for the murder of two young men in rural Putnam County in 1977, but was acquitted by a jury. Also a husband and father, he died in 2007 at age 56, a resident of Shelbyville, Indiana.

Johnny Baniszewski changed his name to John Blake and became a lay pastor in Texas. He married and had children. He died in 2005 of complications of diabetes.

Gertrude Baniszewski changed her name to Nadine Van Fossan while yet in prison, in 1984. She moved to Iowa after her release on parole. She died in 1990 at the age of 62, of lung cancer.

Stephanie Baniszewski went to college and became a teacher in New York state. She married and had children, as did Paula Baniszewski, who moved to Iowa.

Jenny Likens enrolled in the Job Corps in Maine in 1966. She received electronics training and got a computer job at an Indianapolis bank. She died in 2004 at the age of 54. Survivors included two children and a grandchild.

The Likens girls' parents were divorced in 1967. Betty Likens died in 1999 at the age of 71. A clipping of Gertrude Baniszewski's obituary was found among her keepsakes.

Jenny's twin brother, Benny, died four months later in an East Side Indianapolis apartment at age

49, and was cremated at county expense. His father, living in California, learned of the death only months afterward when a letter he wrote the boy was returned marked "Deceased."

James Nedeff died in 1974 at the age of 50. Judge Rabb died in 1976 at age 72. George Rice died in 1991 at age 80. William Erbecker died in 1991 at age 81. Detective Sgt. William Kaiser died in 1991 at age 67. John Hammond died in 1996 at age 69. Leroy New died in 2005 at age 86. Marjorie Wessner left Indianapolis in 1989 to work at the Christian Science headquarters in Boston and is now retired. Forrest Bowman was still practicing law in Indianapolis as of this writing.

The Sylvia Likens case has inspired at least four other literary works: *By Sanction of the Victim*, a novel by Patte Wheat (Major Books, Chatsworth, Calif., 1976); *Hey Rube*, an unpublished play by Janet McReynolds of Boulder, Colo. (and JonBenét Ramsey connections), produced in 1976; *The Basement: Meditations on a Human Sacrifice*, by Kate Millett (Simon & Schuster, New York, 1979), including an imagined narrative by the victim, and *The Girl Next Door*, a novel by Jack Ketchum (Overlook, Woodstock, Ga., 1989). Millett also created sculpture on the theme, shown in a multimedia exhibit at the Noho Gallery on LaGuardia Place, New York, early in 1978.

2008